Frederick William MacMonnies, American, 1863-1937
Diana, c. 1889-90, cast 1917
Bronze, 30⅛ x 21½ x 20½ in.
The Museum of Fine Arts, Houston, museum purchase with funds provided by the Museum Guild in honor of its twentieth anniversary

The *Diana* Underwriters

The Guild of the MFAH expresses sincere thanks to all of the people who so generously contributed to the purchase of Frederick William MacMonnies' *Diana* for the museum's collection in recognition of the twentieth year of the Guild.

Major Benefactor
The Henry K. Roos Family

Benefactors
Deborah and Gary Dunkum
Sheri and Ron Henriksen
Melva and Richard Meronek
Sharon and Brian Olesky

Sponsors
Cathryn Beamon
Terry A. Brown
Marian and Spyros Catechis
Susan Dunn
Jodie Gallagher
Gib Gibbons
Clare A. Glassell
Diane M. Riley

Donors

Margarita Amelio
Angela Rechichi Apollo, M.D.
Sare Aresty
Venetta Armstrong
Peggy Ascherl
Sue Jacobson Bailey
Cleo Barkley
Mr. & Mrs. Jeff L. Barnwell
Mrs. David Bellamy
Deborah Wacker-Bertram
Jeanette Esse Bilbrey
Skip Blakely
Mrs. Gallie N. Bogel
M. Lynne Boughton
Rose Bowles
Mrs. Celina Hellmund Brener
Skip Britton (Mrs. H.L.)
Susanna G. Brundrett
Marjorie H. Capshaw
Grace Manos Catechis
Ralph E. Christensen
Mary Alice Clairborne
Virginia Clark
Robin Singleton Cloyd
Meredith Cocke
Dr. Sandra E. Collazo
Margo Cooper
Elizabeth Copeland
Jenny J. Craig (Mrs. Allen B. III)
Sandra Cravey
Betty Daily
Renee Danziger
Joanne Davee
Aimee de Boisblanc-Kolstad
Robbie deVries
Mrs. Clotaire D. Delery

Ellena P. Dickerson
Susan Tegethoff Diehl
Mrs. Scott R. Dorfman (Laurie)
Mrs. John Jay (Papoose) Douglass
Linda Eyles
Ann Finkelstein
Olivia Fisher
Aline Richardson Freeman
Linda Freiberg
Kathleen Gammill
Mrs. Karl Gautschi
Mary Ann Gilchrist
Susan Goodman
Mrs. Jennifer B. Gordon
Sharon Gordon
Adelma Graham
Jean Grogan
Anne Hailes
Don and Julie Harris
Maggie Hawk
Isabell Smith Herzstein
Penny Hollyfield (Mrs. John S.)
Shirley Holmes
Mrs. Steven F. Hudgins
(Mary-Catherine)
Lillian (Mickie) Huebsch
Lisette Humphrey
Martha and Jordan Hunter
Barbara N. Jackson
Louise Jamail
Carol Kelley
Juanita Kenda
Janet Tarbox Kiersted
Donna Kleist
Ines Kochman-Scott
Constance B. Koomey
Mrs. Chris Krieg (Dawn)
Merrily D. Labarthe
Ruthcelia I. Lane (R.L.)
Susan Lapin
Mrs. Thomas Leger
May and David Litowsky
Mrs. Earl Littman
Kittie Jinkins Livesay
Mrs. James R. Lloyd
Katherine Long
Ann Lyon
JoAnne Maby
Frances Marzio
Jan R. Massaro
Gloria McClure
Amelia H. McDonald
Catherine McNamara
Mitti Meyers
Marilyn Mogas
Bernadine Miller
Alison Mundy
Jeanne Neu
Peg Nevers
Laurie Newendorp
Tassie Nicandros
Mary Ellen O'Brien
Peggy Pennington O'Connor
Barbara Owsley
Susan Patterson
Valerie Peiser
Angela Pesoli Peterman
Mrs. H.A. Ricards, Jr.
Gwen Robberson
Diane Rogers
Judy Camp Sauer
Lois Schroeder
Ann Schultz
Ann L. Schultz
Christina N. Schultz
Martha Ann Selzman
Dotty Shelby
Margaret C. Skidmore
Betty Soph
Bonnie Easterly Spencer
Peggy Henderson Strong
Elsa Swinbank
Martha B. Taylor
Mercedes Riley Terry
Chip and Lynne Thompson
Gloria Thoner
Marguerite Graves Untermeyer
Maaike Van Bemmel
Greta Von Hagge
Bonnie Van Hook
Katherine Veletsos
Pieter and Janet Vrancken
Connie S. Wallace
Jamesene T. Wallace
Shirley Warshaw
Mrs. Donald E. West (Martha)
Patricia Westbrook
Mrs. H. Erwin Wilbanks (Ann)
Audrey Wilkicki
Wilmoth Williams
Catheryn Wilson (Mrs. William N.)
Joyce Winters
Nell Winters
Cyvia G. Wolff
Karen Ytterberg

INTRODUCTION

Fine art and cuisine have always been a masterful combination. At the Museum of Fine Arts, Houston, we delight in the number of artworks that celebrate the pleasures of food and dining in the company of friends and family.

The Guild Collection: Recipes from Art Lovers brings together more than 300 recipes from the museum's family of volunteers and staff. For twenty years, the Guild has generously supported the MFAH through both its hours of service and its gifts for the acquisition of art. This publication is a beautiful and lasting tribute to the Guild's long-standing association with the museum.

Throughout the Guild's cookbook, you will find an amazing variety of recipes to tempt your palate. Complementing the recipes are reproductions of glorious masterworks from the museum collection that span the centuries and showcase world cultures. From a still-life composition to a painting of a bacchanal, the images stir the senses.

I extend my sincere thanks to all of the recipe contributors and testers who helped make this cookbook one to treasure.

Peter C. Marzio
Director
The Museum of Fine Arts, Houston

FOREWORD

In celebration of the Guild's twentieth anniversary, we are pleased to publish *The Guild Collection: Recipes from Art Lovers*. This extraordinary book combines masterworks from the museum collection joined with the culinary creations of Guild members and staff.

The Guild is an organization of volunteers that provides leadership and support to the Museum of Fine Arts, Houston. From the founding of the museum by a group of visionary women in 1900 to the efforts of more than 2,400 individuals today, volunteers have generously given their time and talent to make the MFAH one of the great art museums in the country. Guild members volunteer as docents to provide tours for visitors to the Museum of Fine Arts, Houston, Bayou Bend Collection and Gardens, and Rienzi and assist at the Glassell School of Art. Others help with membership drives, children's parties, programs for families, schools, and senior adults, and a host of behind-the-scenes administrative activities. The Guild membership gives the museum the flexibility to experiment with new initiatives and introduce pilot programs. Proceeds from this cookbook help support the Guild's continuing work at the museum.

Many talented volunteers have contributed their knowledge and time to *The Guild Collection,* and I thank all of them for creating a cookbook that will be treasured for years to come. We also appreciate the staff of the various museum departments, especially rights and reproductions, the registrars office, and publications and graphics, who generously supported us when asked for help. The entire process of this project has been made possible with the hard work and dedication of Janis Odensky, volunteer services coordinator, and Dana Harmier, volunteer administrative assistant. I hope you will use *The Guild Collection* as your guide to entertaining friends and family.

Melva Martinez Meronek
Guild President
1998-1999

F. Bonvin 1861.

COOKBOOK COMMITTEE

Sue Bailey
Deborah Dunkum
Melva Meronek
Sharon Olesky
Valerie Peiser
Connie Wallace

Special Thanks

Chantal Duvall
Olivia Fisher
Sharon Gordon
Dana Harmier
Donna Kleist
Janis Odensky
Margaret C. Skidmore

Francois Bonvin, French, 1817-1887
The Cook, 1861
Charcoal and black chalk on laid paper, $16\frac{1}{16}$ x $12\frac{1}{8}$ in.
The Museum of Fine Arts, Houston, museum purchase with funds provided by the Houston Alumnae Chapter of Delta Delta Delta

Although Bonvin was primarily a painter, this is a fully realized, independent work, not a study for a painting. The concept of creating independent drawings was only about one hundred years old at that time. Bonvin was a leading exponent of the Realist School in mid-nineteenth century France. The Cook is a genre drawing, a scene of everyday life. It is not to be confused with a portrait drawing, as the artist intended to depict a type, not a specific person, even if created with a live model.

Contributors

The Guild of the Museum of Fine Arts, Houston, gratefully acknowledges those members who have contributed their time, talent, and expertise by sharing, testing, proofreading and editing over 500 treasured recipes. The generous efforts of these volunteers have made this publication possible and we sincerely appreciate their contributions.

Leslie Abuso
Holly Anderson
Thelma H Anneler
Angela Apollo
Peggy Ascherl
Sue Bailey
Arvis Barlow
Penny Basnight
Doug Bateman
Carla Belcher
Pamela Bergman
Karen Blansfield
Judy B. Bond
Rose Bowles
Mary "Skip" Britton
Terry Brown
Sue Burrow
Marjorie Capshaw
Chiche Casarsa
Barbara Catechis
Marian Catechis
Mary-Catherine Clark
June Clifford
Laura Cloud
Alexander Cocke
Meredith Cocke
Paula Christie Cohen
Connie Colley
Cindy Cook
Elizabeth Copeland
Patricia Daniel
Beryl Davis
Carolyn N. Davis
Aimee de Boisblanc-Kolstad
Verena Dettwiler
Robbie deVries
Ellena Dickerson
Susan Diehl
Laurie Dorfman
Marilyn Dorries
Deborah Dunkum
Susan Dunn
Chantal Duvall
Pati Mengden-Eckhardt
Dee Elliot
Vicky Nicandros Elliot
Ann Epperson
Orna Feinstein
Olivia Fisher
Sydney LaDell Fredrickson
Linda Freiberg
Melissa Garza
Patricia Gatto
Lotty Gautschi
Kari Gonzales
Beth Goodner
Sharon Gordon
Adelma Graham
Rosalie Green
Alison de Lima Greene
Anne Hailes and Family
Martha Hall
Jane Hanson
Dana Harmier
Julie Harris
Maria Areopauita Harvey
Hallie Harwell
Lesa Hepburn
Rosann Hooks
Martha Hunter
Barbara Jackson
Louise Jamail
Anne Johnson
Peggy Johnson

Jessica Kagan
Melinda Kaltenbacher
Juanita E. Kenda
Janet Kiersted
Kate Kirkland
Donna Kleist
Susan Knight
Eva Korentayer
Merrily LaBarthe
Lucy Lamm
Barbara Leflar
Ruth Lewis
Carolyn Lightfoot
Molly Lindsey
Cindy Linn
Julie Longmore
Tina M. Llorente
Helen Luntz
Bobby Lyall
Ann Lyon
Martha Amdur Malev
Masterson Family
Peter C. Marzio
Beverly Maurice
Amy Mayer
Cathy McNamara
Grace McIlvaine
Ileana Meijide
Melva Martinez Meronek
Mitti Meyers
Julia Miller
Dee Murtaugh
Sue Nardi
Emily Ballew Neff
Peggy Nevers
Laurie Newendorp
Peggy O'Connor
Janis Odensky
Lona Odum
Theda Ogg
Sharon Olesky
Kipper Oyanguren
Janet Patterson
Susan Patterson
Jan Patton
Valerie Peiser
Gooloo Polad
Jean Radelat
Marilyn Ragsdale
Sharon Rankin
Ulla Reichhardt
Eleanor Ricards
Louise Rice
Diane Riley
Gwen Robberson
Trisha Roberts
Jacquelyne M. Rocan
Sybil Roos
Susan Scott Ross
Mary Russell
Heather Sandall
Anne-Louise Schaffer
Petty Schoelman
Lois Schroeder
Ann L. Schultz
Martha Schumacher
Ines I. Kochman-Scott
Teressa Sherrill
Caroline Skelly
Margaret C. Skidmore
Betty Soph
Mary Southwell
Demi Strawman
Kathie Streeter
Helen Sullivan
Vera Svalgaard
Barbara Tartt
Jarnell Elaine Thomas
Lynne Thompson
Cindy Thorp
Patricia Francis Thrash
Jackie Turk
Margarite Untermeyer
Maaike Van Bemmel
Bonnie Van Hook
Virginia Van Horn
Frank Varner
Melissa Varner
E. Therio Vekris
Katherine Veletsos
Greta Von Hagge
Jean Von Rosenberg
Janet Vrancken
Remy Wagner
Connie Wallace
Shirley Warshaw
Carolee Weber
Dotty Wells
Martha West
Karen Whitaker
Stuart Williams
Wilmoth L. Williams
Catheryn Wilson
Nell Winters
Joyce Winters
Amber York
Karen Ytterberg
Del Zimmerman

HISTORY OF THE GUILD

Volunteers have played a key role in the activities and programs of the MFAH since its inception in 1900. This year marks the 20th anniversary of the founding of The Guild, Volunteers of the Museum of Fine Arts Houston, and honors the thousands of dynamic volunteers who have given enthusiastically of their time, energy and resources to make the MFAH a vibrant part of the artistic, cultural and social life of Houston. The following are highlights in the history of The Guild.

1979 Volunteers create The Associates, a membership organization, "to serve the MFAH and to foster interest in the museum." More than 700 members join the first year. They serve as Gallery Guides and support staff for the Annual Contributors Fund, museum school and administrative offices; help run the reception desk; provide hospitality at receptions, and serve as hostesses for the Tea Room.

1980 The Associates Tea Room hostesses begin a cookbook project.

1983 *Treasures from the Shanghai Museum: 6,000 Years of Chinese Art* is the museum's first ticketed exhibition and its most ambitious. The Associates spend more than 6,000 hours staffing the museum's first exhibition retail shop, organizing the first speakers' bureau and managing a crowd of 249,000 visitors.

Houston Fine Arts Cookbook is published.

1984 A new Associate Docent group is created and Gallery Guides are renamed Senior Docents. Associate Docents, Senior Docents and Junior League Docents combine forces for training, providing increased opportunities for mentoring and greater flexibility for the touring program.

Weekend and evening volunteer positions are offered for working professionals.

Christie's Appraisal Day is coordinated by the Associates for museum members.

The Associates changes its name to The Guild of the Museum of Fine Arts, Houston.

Guild volunteers play an important role in the annual Glassell Benefit.

1985 Lobby Desk volunteers take on added responsibilities. Museum hires first full-time Volunteer Services Director.

1986 Guild volunteers organize the first Pumpkin Time in the new Sculpture Garden, the first Children's Holiday Party, the first Holiday Market, and the first Spring Clearance Sale for the museum shops.

The Guild assumes responsibility for the Post-Race Party for the annual Fine Arts 5K Run.

1989 The Guild celebrates its 10th anniversary. Thanks to a special fundraising campaign organized by The Guild, *The Museum of Fine Arts, Houston: A Permanent Legacy* is published.

1990 Museum establishes Henry K. Roos Volunteer Service Award in memory of long time volunteer, Henry Roos. Awarded each year by the museum staff to a volunteer who has given dedicated regular volunteer service for at least five years.

Museum hosts dignitaries attending the Economic Summit of Industrialized Nations and Guild volunteers staff the cultural booth at the George R. Brown Convention Center and the Media party at the museum.

Rediscovering Pompeii attracts more than 352,000 visitors. Guild volunteers run the day-to-day operation of the exhibition.

1991 Record 730,000 people visit the MFAH during the year and membership grows making it among the nation's top ten in terms of attendance. Bayou Bend closes for a two-year renovation and the Bayou Bend Collection of Americana opens to the public at Tenneco.

Guild volunteers serve as hosts for the first Fine Arts Mixer.

1994 The Guild provides orientation for Discovery Through Art classes and assists with the Glassell Junior School's Sketch Day. Volunteer Office moves to new Administration and Junior School Building.

1996 Guild Spring Luncheon previews Rienzi: A Collection of European Decorative Arts, as it begins renovation in preparation of becoming a new addition to the MFAH.

1997 Guild members paint a triptych mural based on the museum's magnificent Tiffany stained-glass window for the construction site around the Beck Building.

1998 Guild organizes first successful artful day trip to San Antonio as a pilot.

Guild recognized on Donor Wall for contributing over 5 million volunteer hours since 1900, the equivalent of over $7.5 million given to the Museum of Fine Arts, Houston.

Holiday Coffee honors Charter Members.

1999 First class of Rienzi Docents completes training. Rienzi opens for the River Oaks Garden Club's annual Azalea Trail, then permanently opens on May 1, 1999.

To celebrate its 20th anniversary, The Guild purchases *Diana*, a bronze sculpture by Frederick William MacMonnies; launches a cookbook project, and presents the 100-year history of the MFAH and its volunteers in a special museum exhibition, *The Art of Volunteering: Celebrating the Twentieth Anniversary of The Guild.*

2000 Audrey Jones Beck Building opens. Many new volunteer opportunities are created. This new building more than doubles the museum's program and exhibition space and raises the museum's rank among U.S. art museums from 30th to 6th in terms of exhibition space.

TABLE OF CONTENTS

Appetizer & Beverage Collection	17
Bread & Brunch Collection	51
Soup, Salad & Sauce Collection	71
Pasta & Casserole Collection	113
Vegetable Collection	123
Meat Collection	139
Poultry & Seafood Collection	165
Dessert Collection	189
Cooking Tips	238
Index	245

Auguste Renoir, French, 1841-1919
A Girl Reading, 1890
Oil on canvas, 13¼ x 16¼ in.
The Museum of Fine Arts, Houston, gift of Audrey Jones Beck

As one of the founding members of the Impressionist group, Renoir was known for his paintings of voluptuous women and charming portraits of children. He was fascinated by the innocence of childhood and captured this freshness and animation with a subtle delicacy. This young girl reads quietly against a backdrop of rich and voluminous fabric, painted with a tenderness and warmth that characterizes Renoir's best work. On the subject of paintings he stated, "To my mind a picture should be something agreeable, cheerful – and yes! Nice to look at."

APPETIZER & BEVERAGE COLLECTION

Akan
Africa, Ghana
Sword Ornament in the Shape of a Teapot, c. 1920
Cast gold, 5⅝ x 6¾ in.
The Museum of Fine Arts, Houston, the Glassell Collection of African Gold, gift of Alfred C. Glassell, Jr.

This sword ornament of cast gold in the shape of a teapot shows the adaptation of motifs from a British silver service. Its small and delicate shape and elaborate filigree gold belie its significance as part of the traditions of the Asante people of Ghana. Placed on the hilt of an ornamental sword, it would be carried by a specially appointed bearer of the Asantehene on important ceremonial and state occasions signifying the authority of the chief and assuring the continuity of the lineage and bloodline of the chief. The world-renown Glassell Collection of African Gold dates from the late nineteenth to early twentieth century and represents the mastery of the goldsmiths of the Akan nations, especially perfecting the lost-wax process.

Appetizer & Beverage Collection

Caviar Pie
Pirkko's Caviar
Zack's Cream Cheese Torte
Karen's Raspberry Cheese Spread
Aimee's Artichoke and Sun-Dried Tomato Dip
Artichoke Dip
Ham-Asparagus Roll-Ups
Asparagus Appetizers
Zucchini Nibbles
Corn Walnut Dip
Pickle Mushrooms à la Grecque
Olive Nut Spread
Curried Cheese and Olive Spread
Olive Cheese Nuggets
Almond Swiss Cheese Ball
Pinecone Cheese Ball
Goat Cheese with Sun-Dried Tomatoes and Rosemary
Baked Spinach Square
Greek Spinach Appetizer
Baked Brie with Crudités
Texas Caviar
Tortilla Roll-Ups
Jalapeño Cheese Bites
Jalapeño Squares
Pizza Rustica
Chutney Cheese Pâté
Tapenade Dip
Shrimp de Jonghe
Karen's Shrimp Dip
Shrimp Spread
Southwestern Salmon Spirals
Capanada
My Great Aunt Willimae's King Salmon Mold
Smoked Oyster Spread
Alexander's* Smoked Salmon or Ham Roll-Ups
"Smoked" Salmon Spread
Cheese Straws
Debbye's Chicken Log Appetizer
Pastelitos
Venison Tenderloin Appetizers

Hot Gingered Lemonade
Brandied Mocha
Champagne with Raspberries
Holiday Champagne Punch
Café Brulot
Christmas Tea
Festive Party Punch
Ginger Almond Tea
Kentucky Christmas Cider
Eggnog No. 302
Lemony-Light Cooler
Mint Syrup Concentrate
Sangría
Jalapeño Margaritas
Sparkling Strawberry Punch
Cranberry Glogg

CAVIAR PIE

6 chopped hard-cooked eggs
3 tablespoons mayonnaise
1 medium sweet red onion, chopped
1 (8 ounce) package cream cheese
⅔ cup sour cream
1 jar lumpfish caviar (drained)

Combine eggs and mayonnaise. Spread in bottom of well-greased 8-inch springform pan. Sprinkle with chopped onion. Combine cream cheese and sour cream and beat until smooth. Drop by spoonfuls on the eggs and onions and spread until covered. Chill 3 hours or overnight. Just before serving, top with caviar, spreading to the edge of pan. Run knife around side to loosen. Lift off springform pan side. Serve with pumpernickel bread.

Yield: 6 servings.

PIRKKO'S CAVIAR

2 pints whipping cream
1 medium red onion, finely chopped
1 jar caviar (red preferred), drained

Whip cream until fairly stiff. Fold in onion and caviar, lightly. Serve in extravagant crystal bowl, with small knife for applying this rich delicacy to small crackers or Melba rounds.

Yield: 12 servings.

ZACK'S CREAM CHEESE TORTE

3 pounds cream cheese
1 cup chopped pecans
1 cup bell peppers, green and/or red
1 cup chopped white onion
1 (16 ounce) can crushed pineapple, wrung out very dry
1 tablespoon seasoned salt

Mix all ingredients. Put in round spring pan lined with plastic wrap. Chill in refrigerator, one hour minimum. Unmold, decorate with more crushed pecans around side, rosettes of cream cheese around edge with pepper piece center. Serve with crackers.

Yield: 12 servings.

KAREN'S RASPBERRY CHEESE SPREAD

1½ pounds grated sharp cheddar cheese
½ cup chopped onion
½ cup chopped pecans
¼ cup mayonnaise
¼ teaspoon red cayenne pepper
Dash hot pepper sauce
Raspberry jam

Mix all ingredients except raspberry jam together. It will mix easier if kneaded by hand. Put into a 9 inch tart pan with removable bottom. Chill overnight in refrigerator. Before serving, remove from pan and spread top with jam. Serve with lots of crackers.

Yield: 48 servings.

AIMEE'S ARTICHOKE AND SUN-DRIED TOMATO DIP

1/4 cup freshly shredded Parmesan cheese
1/2 cup sour cream
1/2 cup mayonnaise
1/2 cup coarsely chopped sun-dried tomatoes (oil-packed or dried, softened)
2 cups Swiss cheese, shredded
1 (14 ounce) can artichoke hearts, drained and chopped
1/4 teaspoon garlic powder
1/4 teaspoon hot pepper sauce
Chopped fresh parsley, if desired
Crackers, toasted baguette slices or bread sticks

Heat oven to 350°. In a large bowl, stir together all ingredients except parsley and crackers. Spoon into 9 inch oven-proof shallow dish. Bake 22 to 26 minutes or until edges are very lightly browned. Sprinkle with parsley. Serve with crackers, baguettes or bread sticks.

Hint: To soften sun-dried tomatoes, cover tomatoes with boiling water. Let stand 5 to 10 minutes, drain.

Yield: 6 to 8 servings.

ARTICHOKE DIP

1 can artichoke hearts, packed in oil, drained and chopped
3/4 cup mayonnaise
1/4 cup grated Parmesan cheese
1 teaspoon lemon juice
3-4 garlic cloves

Heat oven to 350°. In medium bowl, combine hearts, mayonnaise, Parmesan cheese, lemon juice and garlic. Spread in ungreased 9 inch quiche plate. Bake at 350° for 20 to 25 minutes or until thoroughly heated. Serve hot with crackers or vegetable dippers.

Yield: 2½ cups.

HAM-ASPARAGUS ROLL-UPS

1 pound asparagus
12 ounces whipped cream cheese
26 ounces thinly sliced cooked ham (rectangular shaped)
You will need one slice of ham for each asparagus spear

Wash and trim asparagus spears. Place in a microwave-safe bowl with 2 tablespoons of water. Cover with lid or plastic wrap and vent. Microwave on high for about 2 minutes or until crisp-tender. Drain and plunge in cold water. Drain. Spread a thin layer of cream cheese, about 1½ tablespoons, on each slice of ham. Place one spear of asparagus on the ham and roll tightly. Slice into 4 pieces and secure each with a toothpick.

Yield: approximately 100 pieces.

ASPARAGUS APPETIZERS

3 ounces blue cheese
1 (8 ounce) package cream cheese
1 egg
20 asparagus spears
20 slices honey-wheat bread
¼ cup butter, melted
⅛ teaspoon cayenne pepper, optional
¼ teaspoon garlic salt, optional

Mix softened cheese well, stir in beaten egg. Trim crusts from bread and roll out with rolling pin. Spread cheese mixture on one slice at a time, place cooked asparagus spear (or a canned spear) at front of edge of slice and roll up. Repeat with remaining slices. Brush each roll with melted butter and cut into thirds and place on cookie sheet. Bake 10 to 12 minutes in preheated 400° oven.

Hint: Can be frozen before baking and removed from freezer when needed.

Yield: 40 to 60 servings.

ZUCCHINI NIBBLES

Fresh zucchini, cut into julienne (matchstick size and shape)
Buttermilk
Flour
Lemon pepper
Grated Parmesan cheese

Soak the zucchini in the buttermilk, then dredge them in the flour. Shake off the excess flour, and drop into very hot oil. When done, remove and drain on paper towel. Sprinkle the cooked zucchini with lemon pepper and Parmesan cheese.

Yield: 4 to 6 servings.

CORN WALNUT DIP

2 (8 ounce) packages cream cheese
¼ cup fresh lemon juice
1 teaspoon salt
1 teaspoon pepper
1 teaspoon cayenne pepper
1 tablespoon cumin
1 (8 ounce) can whole kernel corn, drained
1 cup chopped walnuts
3 green onions, chopped
1 (4 ounce) can green chiles, chopped (do not drain)

Bring cream cheese to room temperature. Whip with electric mixer until fluffy. Beat in seasonings. Stir in corn, walnuts, green onions, and green chiles with their liquid. Serve with tortilla chips.

Yield: 2 cups.

PICKLE MUSHROOMS À LA GRECQUE

2 pounds mushrooms (medium-sized)
¼ teaspoon thyme leaves
3 whole peppercorns
¼ teaspoon fennel seeds
2 bay leaves
1 teaspoon garlic powder
2 teaspoons onion powder
6 tablespoons red wine vinegar
4 tablespoons olive oil
1 teaspoon lemon peel
6 teaspoons Beau Monde seasoning
1 tablespoon parsley

Wash mushrooms in cold water. Pat dry. Crush thyme leaves, peppercorns and fennel seed. Combine in sauce pan. Add next 8 ingredients. Cook over low heat, turning mushrooms often, until they are tender (about 15 minutes). Pour mushrooms and marinade into glass jars and refrigerate. Chill several hours. Mushrooms will keep two weeks in refrigerator.

Yield: 12 servings.

OLIVE NUT SPREAD

1 (6 ounce) package cream cheese, softened
½ cup mayonnaise
2 tablespoons liquid from salad olives
Dash of ground pepper
½ cup chopped pecans
1 cup chopped green salad olives

Combine the cream cheese and mayonnaise in a medium bowl and mix well. Add the liquid from the salad olives and the pepper and mix. Fold in the pecans and the salad olives. Chill.

Yield: 10 servings.

CURRIED CHEESE AND OLIVE SPREAD

¼ cup chopped ripe olives
⅓ cup chopped green onions
½ cup mayonnaise
2 cups sharp cheddar grated
½ teaspoon curry powder
½ cup chopped pecans, optional

Combine all ingredients. Spread on buttered toasted bread rounds. Bake 10 minutes at 350°.

Yield: 3 cups.

OLIVE CHEESE NUGGETS

1 cup shredded sharp cheddar cheese
¼ cup soft butter
¾ cup sifted flour
⅛ teaspoon salt
½ teaspoon paprika
1 bottle stuffed green olives

Mix cheese and soft butter and add flour, salt and paprika. Shape the mixed dough around medium sized stuffed green olives. Use about 1 teaspoon of dough for each olive. Place on an ungreased baking sheet. Bake at 400° for 12 to 15 minutes. Serve hot or cold. This recipe can be refrigerated overnight before baking.

Yield: 24 pieces.

ALMOND SWISS CHEESE BALL

- 1 (8 ounce) package Swiss cheese
- 1 (8 ounce) package cream cheese, softened
- 3 tablespoons butter
- ½ teaspoon almond extract
- 2 tablespoons amaretto liqueur
- 1 (2 ounce) package sliced almonds
- Crackers

Use steel blade of food processor. Start with Swiss cheese and process ingredients (except almonds) in order listed. Form into ball and chill. Toast almonds in 300° oven. When ready to serve, roll cheese ball in toasted sliced almonds and serve with crackers.

Yield: 8 servings.

PINECONE CHEESE BALL

- 1 (8 ounce) container garden vegetable cream cheese
- 1 (8 ounce) container roasted garlic cream cheese
- 1 cup (4 ounces) shredded sharp cheddar cheese
- 3 green onions, chopped
- 2 cups pecan halves, toasted
- Fresh rosemary sprigs
- ½ teaspoon parsley
- ¼ teaspoon seasoned salt

Stir together cheeses, onion, parsley and seasoned salt. Shape into an oval. Chill 2 hours. Arrange pecan halves over cheese oval in overlapping rows beginning at the bottom and working upward to resemble a pinecone. Arrange rosemary sprigs at top of pinecone, sticking stems into top of cheese pinecone to resemble leaves coming out of the top. Serve with crackers.

Yield: 20 servings.

GOAT CHEESE WITH SUN-DRIED TOMATOES AND ROSEMARY

Marinated Tomatoes

8 sun-dried tomatoes, packed in oil
3 cloves garlic, minced
2 tablespoons olive oil
1 tablespoon chopped fresh or dried rosemary
¼ cup diced fresh tomatoes
2 tablespoons minced parsley, fresh
2 tablespoons prepared pesto sauce

Base

1 baguette
Olive oil
6 ounce goat cheese
Fresh rosemary sprigs

Chop the sun-dried tomatoes. Combine with next 6 ingredients. Cover and chill up to 4 hours. Slice baguette thinly. Drizzle with the additional olive oil. Place the baking sheet with the rounds in a 350° oven for 8 minutes, or until crisp and slightly toasted. Just before serving, place the goat cheese (set out of the refrigerator for 30 minutes) on a serving plate and top with marinated tomatoes and surround with the baguette rounds.

Yield: 1 cup.

BAKED SPINACH SQUARE

1 (10 ounce) package frozen chopped spinach
3 slices crisp bacon, crumbled
1 can condensed cream of pablano soup
2 eggs, slightly beaten
⅓ cup packaged herb dressing mix
¼ teaspoon cayenne pepper
3 white mushrooms, coarsely chopped

Cook spinach without salt. Drain. Combine with other ingredients. Bake at 350° for 35 minutes.

Hint: Cook in a ring mold. Then fill center with curried rice when baked spinach has been turned out on a serving plate. It makes a great combination of flavors.

Yield: 8 servings.

GREEK SPINACH APPETIZER

1 (10 ounce) package frozen chopped spinach, drained
1 Roma tomato, finely chopped
¼ cup chopped onions
1 large garlic clove, minced
¼ cup mayonnaise
¼ cup sour cream
½ teaspoon dill weed
¼ teaspoon salt
1 baguette, sliced ¼ inch thick

Defrost spinach, drain and press out all liquid. Mix first 8 ingredients together thoroughly. Place a tablespoon of mix on each round. Bake approximately 15 minutes in a 325° oven.

Yield: 12 servings.

BAKED BRIE WITH CRUDITÉS

2 tablespoons unsalted butter
1 large onion, chopped
2 tablespoons minced garlic
8 ounces Brie cheese, rind trimmed, cheese cut into pieces
1 (8 ounce) package cream cheese, cut into pieces
¾ cup sour cream
2 teaspoon fresh lemon juice
2 teaspoon brown sugar
1 teaspoon Worcestershire sauce
1 (18 ounce) round sourdough bread loaf
Paprika
Assorted crudités (such as zucchini rounds, broccoli and cauliflower florets, carrot and bell pepper sticks) or cubed bread from inside sourdough loaf

Melt 2 tablespoons unsalted butter in heavy medium skillet over medium heat. Add onion and garlic and sauté until onion is golden brown, about 10 minutes. Set aside. Place Brie and cream cheese in large microwave-safe bowl. Microwave on medium just until melted, about 2 minutes. Whisk in onion mixture, sour cream, fresh lemon juice, brown sugar and Worcestershire sauce. Cut off top of bread loaf. Scoop out center of loaf, leaving ¾ inch thick shell of bread. Spoon cheese mixture into loaf. Place bread lid atop loaf. Wrap in foil. (Can be prepared 1 day ahead; refrigerate. When ready to use, let stand 2 hours at room temperature before baking.) Preheat oven to 400°. Bake loaf until filling bubbles, about 1 hour. Unwrap and place on platter. Remove bread lid. Sprinkle cheese mixture with paprika. Serve with crudités.

Hint: Slice bread shell and toast later for a "cheese sandwich".

Yield: 8 servings.

TEXAS CAVIAR

4 cups black-eyed peas, drained
1 (16 ounce) can white hominy, drained
1-2 medium tomatoes, chopped
1 cup Italian salad dressing
½ cup chopped onion
4 green onions, sliced
1-2 jalapeño peppers, seeded and chopped
1-2 cloves garlic, minced
1 cup chopped green pepper

In a large bowl, combine all ingredients, cover, and chill for 1 or 2 days.

Yield: 8 servings.

TORTILLA ROLL-UPS

6-8 large flour tortillas
2 (8 ounce) packages cream cheese, softened
1 (4 ounce) can chopped green chiles
1 (4 ounce) can chopped ripe olives
3-4 chopped green onions
Picante sauce, optional

Combine cream cheese, chiles, olive and onions. Spread on tortillas. Roll up and wrap in plastic wrap. Refrigerate up to several days. Before serving, slice into ½ inch pieces. Serve with picante sauce for dipping, if desired.

Yield: 90 pieces.

JALAPEÑO CHEESE BITES

1 (8 ounce) jar jalapeño slices
1 pound grated cheddar cheese
6 eggs
1½ cups cooked white rice
1 (2 ounce) jar of pimentos

Preheat oven to 250°. Grease a 9 X 13 inch baking dish. Drain and chop jalapeño slices. Cover the bottom of the pan with jalapeño pieces. Stir cheese and eggs in a large bowl. Add rice, stir well. Add pimentos, stir well. Pour mixture over jalapeño pieces. Bake at 250° for 1 hour. Allow to cool, cut into 1 inch squares.

Yield: 10 dozen.

JALAPEÑO SQUARES

1 small can jalapeños
1 pound grated cheddar cheese
10 large or 12 medium eggs
¼ cup diced onion
Salsa, optional

Spray a 9 X 13 inch pan with non-stick spray. Spread peppers in a single layer. Sprinkle with cheese and onion. Top with beaten eggs. Bake at 350° for 20 to 30 minutes. Cool and cut into squares. Serve with salsa, if desired.

PIZZA RUSTICA

1 package hot rolls mix
1 (15 ounce) container whole milk ricotta
1 (8 ounce) shredded whole milk mozzarella
½ cup grated Parmigiano-Reggiano or Asiago or kasseri cheese
¼ pound Genoa salami, diced
⅓ cup sliced green onions
3 tablespoons chopped parsley
1 teaspoon oregano
1 teaspoon salt
3 eggs, slightly beaten, divided

Prepare roll mix according to directions. Let stand in an oiled bowl for 30 minutes or until it doubles in volume. Mix other ingredients (save out approximately 2 tablespoons of the eggs). Punch dough down. Divide in two equal parts. Oil a 12 inch pie dish. Stretch ½ of the pizza dough over the pan, make an edge. Spoon filling over the dough. Roll the remaining dough, fit it over the filling and press the edges together. Prick the entire surface with a 2-prong fork. If you wish, cut some decorations from the trimmings. Brush the top with the eggs set aside. Decorate the top and brush the decorations. Bake in a 350° oven for about 1 hour or until the top is golden brown. Cover the top with foil if the pizza is browning too fast. Let stand 15 minutes before cutting.

Hint: This pizza can be made in advance and it is very good at room temperature. You can serve it as a meal accompanied by a salad, or cut into small pieces for an appetizer. It is great for a buffet.

Yield: 8 servings.

CHUTNEY CHEESE PÂTÉ

2 (3 ounce) package cream cheese, softened
1 cup sharp cheddar cheese, grated
4 teaspoons dry sherry
½ teaspoon curry powder
1 (8 ounce) jar chutney
2-3 green onions, with tops, chopped

Beat first 4 ingredients by hand. Shape into block about ½ inch thick. Chill. When ready to serve, top with chutney and green onions.

Yield: 6 servings.

TAPENADE DIP

1 cup pitted kalamata olives
1 cup fresh basil leaves
6 anchovy fillets
2 tablespoons drained capers
2 garlic cloves, coarsely chopped
1 tablespoon fresh lemon juice
½ cup mayonnaise
Salt and pepper

Blend all ingredients except mayonnaise in processor until finely chopped. Transfer to small bowl. Mix in mayonnaise. Season to taste with salt and pepper. Can be prepared 3 days ahead, cover and refrigerate. Serve with slices of French bread or vegetables.

Yield: 8 to 10 servings.

SHRIMP DE JONGHE

1 cup butter, melted
2 cloves garlic, minced
⅓ cup chopped parsley
½ teaspoon paprika
Dash cayenne
⅔ cup cooking sherry or white wine
2 cups soft bread crumbs
5-6 cups cleaned cooked shrimp (4 pounds in shell)

Melt butter and add next 5 ingredients. Add breadcrumbs and toss. Place cleaned shrimp in a 11 X 7 X 1½ inch baking dish. Spoon the butter mixture over. Bake at 325° for 20 to 25 minutes or till crumbs brown. Sprinkle with more chopped parsley.

Yield: 16 to 20 servings.

KAREN'S SHRIMP DIP

1 (8 ounce) package cream cheese
8 ounces Thousand Island salad dressing
½ cup mayonnaise
1 small onion, grated
2 pounds cooked shrimp, chopped
¼ cup minced green onions
3 teaspoons hot pepper sauce
1 tablespoon season salt
1 tablespoon horseradish

Cream the cream cheese with dressing and mayonnaise. Stir in remaining ingredients. Chill and serve with crackers or chips.

Yield: 12 servings.

SHRIMP SPREAD

¾ cup celery, chopped fine
½ cup onions, chopped fine
1 can tomato soup
2 small cans shrimp, drained
1 cup mayonnaise
2 (8 ounce) packages cream cheese
1½ envelopes unflavored gelatin

Heat soup in saucepan on low heat. Melt in the cream cheese, stirring constantly. Cool for 5 minutes. Dissolve the gelatin in ½ cup of boiling water, add to other ingredients and mix thoroughly. Pour into mold and refrigerate for 4 to 5 hours. Remove from mold and serve with small snack crackers.

Hint: Use a fish mold.

Yield: 8 to 10 servings.

SOUTHWESTERN SALMON SPIRALS

3 tablespoons cilantro, finely chopped
10 ounces goat cheese, room temperature
24 ounces smoked salmon, thinly sliced
Juice of one lime
Paprika

Mix the cilantro, goat cheese, lime juice and paprika until smooth. Arrange the salmon slices on a sheet of plastic wrap to form an area 12 by 3½ inches. The salmon should be slightly overlapping. Spread the cheese mixture on the salmon sheet leaving about a ½ inch border of salmon. Lift the plastic wrap on the long side and roll the salmon into a log shape. Repeat until all the salmon has been used. Refrigerate until ready to serve. Once ready to serve, remove the plastic wrap and slice the salmon into ¾ inch pieces. Dust lightly with paprika before serving.

Yield: 25 servings.

CAPANADA

2 large eggplants, peeled and coarsely chopped
3 cups onion, coarsely chopped
1½ cups bell pepper, coarsely chopped
1½ cups celery, coarsely chopped
½ cup olive oil
1 (8 ounce) can tomato sauce
1 (8 ounce) can tomato paste
1 clove garlic, minced
½ cup pine nuts
1 (6 ounce) can pitted black olives, whole
½ cup pitted green olives, whole
½ cup red wine vinegar
3 tablespoons sugar
½ cup capers
1½ teaspoons oregano
1 tablespoon salt
1 teaspoon cayenne pepper
1 teaspoon pepper

Soak eggplant in salt water for 20 minutes and drain. In a 4 quart microwavable casserole, sauté onion, bell pepper and celery in olive oil. Cover with paper and cook on high 30 minutes. Stir once or twice. Stir in eggplant. Cover and cook on high for 30 minutes. Stir once. Add tomato sauce and paste. Cook on high 10 minutes. Stir in garlic, pine nuts, olives, vinegar, sugar, capers, oregano, salt, and peppers. Cook on high 5 minutes. Chill before serving.

Hint: Serve with crackers or slices of French bread. Will keep 3 weeks in refrigerator.

Yield: 8 to 10 servings.

MY GREAT AUNT WILLIMAE'S KING SALMON MOLD

1 pound salmon (can use canned, reserve liquid)
½ cup finely chopped celery
¼ cup minced onion
½ teaspoon dill weed, optional
2 packages unflavored gelatin
½ cup cold water
½ cup catsup
¼ cup vinegar
Dash hot pepper sauce, optional
1 cup mayonnaise

Drain salmon, reserve liquid. Flake salmon. Mix with celery, onion and dill, if desired. Soften gelatin in water. Combine reserved salmon liquid, catsup, vinegar and hot pepper sauce, if desired; bring to a boil. Add softened gelatin. Stir until dissolved. Gently blend hot liquid with salmon mixture. Stir in mayonnaise. Turn into 1 quart fish mold, which has been coated with additional mayonnaise. Chill until firm.

Hint: If desired, sprinkle with paprika and use stuffed olive slices for eyes and a sprig of parsley for a tail. Garnish with deviled eggs, tomato quarters, green onions, pickles, carrot sticks, olives, and pickled beets.

Yield: 20 appetizer servings or 6 to 8 as main dish.

SMOKED OYSTER SPREAD

2 (8 ounce) packages of cream cheese, softened
2 tins smoked oysters, rinsed and chopped
2-3 teaspoons Worcestershire sauce
3 tablespoons grated onion
1 clove garlic, minced
2-3 tablespoons mayonnaise
Salt
Dash of hot pepper sauce

Mix all ingredients together and serve. Garnish with parsley. Chill overnight.

Yield: 2 cups.

ALEXANDER'S* SMOKED SALMON OR HAM ROLL-UPS

4 ounces smoked salmon or sliced ham
Grated provolone cheese
Minced walnuts or pecans

Take 1 slice salmon or ham and cover with layer of cheese and layer of nuts. Roll up this slice of salmon/ham like a jelly roll. Slice roll into appetizer portions. Spear with a toothpick. Repeat with remaining salmon or ham. Arrange on a plate and serve.

*10-year-old Alexander submitted this for other kids to make.

Yield: 20 servings.

"SMOKED" SALMON SPREAD

1 (7½ ounce) can red salmon, drained
1 (8 ounce) package cream cheese
1 tablespoon grated onion
2 teaspoons lemon juice
¾ teaspoon liquid smoke
½ teaspoon Worcestershire sauce
3 dashes hot pepper sauce
Snipped parsley
Crackers or small rye bread rounds

Break apart salmon and remove any large bones and any large pieces of skin. Blend cream cheese and salmon thoroughly. Add remaining ingredients and beat. Put in serving bowl and sprinkle snipped parsley on top. Serve with crackers or bread.

Yield: 8 servings.

CHEESE STRAWS

1 cup grated sharp cheddar cheese
½ cup butter (not margarine)
1 cup flour
1 egg yolk
Approximately 2 to 3 tablespoons cold water
½-1 teaspoon salt
Paprika

Mix together all ingredients except paprika. Chill. Roll out dough to ⅛ inch thick. Slice into strips. Bake on cookie sheet at 400° for about 10 minutes. When done, sprinkle with paprika. Let cool on wire racks. Store in a tightly covered tin box and they will keep for weeks.

Variation: Dough can be rolled out and cut into biscuits, baking at 400° for about 10 minutes or until lightly browned. If desired, cook with a nut in the center of each one.

Yield: 75 pieces.

DEBBYE'S CHICKEN LOG APPETIZER

½ (8 ounce) package of cream cheese
1 tablespoon chopped chutney
2 tablespoons mayonnaise
1 cup chopped cooked chicken
1 cup chopped almonds
1 tablespoon curry powder
½ cup grated coconut

Blend all ingredients but coconut together. Shape into a log or into balls. Roll in coconut to taste. Serve with crackers.

Hint: Can be made ahead and refrigerated. Spreads more easily when room temperature.

Yield: 2½ cups.

PASTELITOS

Meat Filling

¾ cup green and red peppers, coarsely chopped
1½ tablespoons margarine
2 pounds onions
4 tablespoons butter
2 pounds ground beef
4 tablespoons tomato paste
1 teaspoon dried oregano
1 teaspoon salt
2 teaspoons crushed hot red pepper
1 teaspoon black pepper, freshly ground
1 tablespoon sugar, optional

Fry peppers in margarine, drain and set aside. Chop onions and sauté in butter until translucent. Add ground beef, mix well with onions, turn up the heat and bring to a boil. Add tomato paste. Lower heat and simmer for 30 minutes, stirring occasionally. Add oregano, salt, red pepper, black pepper, and sugar, if desired. Cook for a few more minutes. Remove from the heat, add cooked peppers and allow to cool. Place filling in refrigerator for 24 hours.

Spinach Filling

4 tablespoons margarine
1 cup onions, chopped
3 cups spinach, fresh or frozen, cooked and strained
Salt to taste
Pepper to taste
Nutmeg to taste
¾ cup Parmesan cheese

Cook enough fresh or frozen spinach to make 3 cups after straining. Sauté onions in margarine until translucent. Add spinach, salt, pepper, and nutmeg, to taste. Cook for a few minutes, add Parmesan cheese. Cool.

(continued on next page)

PASTELITOS *(continued)*

PASTRY FOR FRIED PASTELITOS

4 cups all-purpose flour
4 tablespoons butter
3 egg yolks
1½ cups lukewarm water
1 teaspoon salt

Mix in traditional manner or in a food processor. Remove dough from bowl and place in a plastic bag. Let stand for ½ hour. Divide dough into 4 parts. Roll this pastry out very thinly on a floured surface. Cut circles with a 2½ inch cutter. Place a small amount of filling of choice in the center of a circle, cover with another circle and seal the edges with the prongs of a fork. Uncooked pastelitos can be frozen for use later. If planning to freeze put on a baking sheet in the freezer and later transfer the pastelitos to a strong container to prevent breakage. When required, defrost and deep fry. Drain off on paper towels and serve warm.

Hint: Frozen empanada discs are available at some specialty and ethnic markets.

Yield: 8 to 12 pastries.

VENISON TENDERLOIN APPETIZERS

1 venison tenderloin backstrap (1½ to 2 pounds)
¾ cup red wine
3 tablespoons olive oil
2 tablespoons liquid smoke
2 tablespoons Worcestershire sauce
1½ teaspoons cumin seeds
1 teaspoon thyme
2 garlic cloves, minced
1 small onion, minced
¼ teaspoon black pepper
¼ teaspoon cayenne pepper
Assortment of crusty rolls
Spicy mustard and mayonnaise

Trim tenderloin of white membrane. Tie with string to hold together, if necessary. Place in shallow dish. Combine wine, oil, liquid smoke, and Worcestershire sauce and mix well. Add cumin seeds and rest of ingredients and mix well. Pour over tenderloin and cover tightly. Refrigerate at least 4 or 5 hours or overnight. Remove tenderloin, reserve marinade for basting only. Grill tenderloin over medium hot coals for 15 to 20 minutes. Turn once and baste frequently with marinade. Allow meat to stand for 10 minutes. Slice thinly with electric knife. Serve with party rolls, spicy mustard and mayonnaise.

Yield: 15 appetizer servings.

HOT GINGERED LEMONADE

⅔ cup water
2 tablespoons frozen concentrate for lemonade
1½ teaspoons slivered candied ginger
1-2 tablespoons light rum, optional
Lemon slices

Combine ingredients. Heat, uncovered, in a microwave oven until hot, about 1½ minutes. Can use conventional range, heat until simmering. Stir well. Garnish with lemon slice.

Yield: 1 serving.

BRANDIED MOCHA

1 tablespoon instant chocolate-flavored drink powder
2 teaspoons instant coffee powder or granules
2 teaspoons brandy or ½ teaspoon brandy extract
⅔ cup milk
Whipped cream

Combine ingredients. Heat, uncovered, in a microwave oven until hot, about 1½ minutes. Can use conventional range, heat until simmering. Stir and top with whipped cream.

Yield: 1 serving.

CHAMPAGNE WITH RASPBERRIES

24 raspberries, divided
6 teaspoons cognac or other brandy, divided
1½ tablespoons sugar, divided
1 bottle of champagne or other sparkling wine, well chilled, divided

In each of 6 champagne flutes, place 4 berries, 1 teaspoon brandy, and ¼ teaspoon sugar. Mash the raspberries gently with a spoon. Divide the sparkling wine among the glasses and serve immediately.

Yield: 6 servings.

HOLIDAY CHAMPAGNE PUNCH

1 gallon cranberry juice
1 gallon pineapple juice
1 gallon fresh-squeezed orange juice
2 quarts ginger ale
2 (750 ml) bottles champagne (dry)
Orange slices and fresh strawberries for garnish

Combine the juice and ginger ale. Slowly stir in the champagne just before serving. Add ice and garnish with orange slices and strawberries.

Yield: 45 (6 ounce) servings.

CAFÉ BRULOT

16 lumps sugar
12 jiggers cognac
4 sticks of cinnamon
2 twists of lemon peel
24 whole cloves
4 large twists of orange peel
10 demitasse cups of strong coffee
Whipped cream, optional

Place all ingredients except coffee into chafing dish and let stand for 1 hour. Flame for 1 to 2 minutes and slowly add hot coffee. Top with whipped cream if desired.

Yield: 10 servings.

CHRISTMAS TEA

13 cups water, divided
2 cups sugar
4 family sized tea bags
1¼ cups lemon juice
2 tablespoons almond extract
2 teaspoons vanilla

Bring 8 cups of water and sugar to a boil. Add 5 cups water and tea bags. Steep tea for 10 minutes. Add lemon juice, almond extract and vanilla. Can heat and serve hot or chilled and served cold.

Yield: 14 cups.

FESTIVE PARTY PUNCH

2 cups water
2 cups sugar
1 (3 ounce) package of lemon flavored gelatin
1 (6 ounce) can frozen lemonade
1 (6 ounce) can frozen orange juice
1 ounce almond extract
1 (46 ounce) can pineapple juice
3 (2 liter) bottles of diet Sprite

In pan on stove, dissolve water and sugar; Remove from stove. Add gelatin, lemonade, orange juice, pineapple juice and almond extract. Stir until all mixed. Separate into 3 equal amounts and freeze. To serve, thaw each container until slushy, place in punch bowl and add diet Sprite.

Hint: The color of the punch can be changed by using different flavors of gelatin.

Hint: Rinsed, gallon sized milk cartons will work nicely and stack well in the freezer.

Variation: Use lime gelatin and ginger ale.

Yield: 3 to 4 gallons.

GINGER ALMOND TEA

5 cups water, divided
5 regular tea bags
1½ cups sugar
¾ cup lemon juice, fresh or bottled
1 tablespoon vanilla extract
1 teaspoon almond extract
1 (liter) bottle ginger ale

Pour 1 cup of boiling water over tea bags and steep for several minutes. Remove bags. Stir in sugar, 4 cups of water, lemon juice, vanilla extract, and almond extract. Chill. Stir in ginger ale. Serve over ice.

Yield: 3 quarts.

KENTUCKY CHRISTMAS CIDER

1 cup ginger ale
8-10 whole allspice
6-8 whole cloves
1 (8 ounce) package cinnamon red hots
5 sticks of cinnamon
1 gallon apple cider

Mix all ingredients and place over low heat. Heat well but do not boil. Strain and serve.

Yield: 18 to 36 servings.

EGGNOG NO. 302

⅔ cup sugar
4 eggs, separated
⅓ cup rum
⅓ cup bourbon
½ pint milk
2 teaspoons vanilla extract
1 pint whipping cream
Nutmeg, optional

Separate egg yolks and whites. Set whites aside in refrigerator. Combine egg yolks, sugar, rum and bourbon. Stir well with mixer. Set aside in refrigerator for at least 2 hours. Add milk and vanilla to mixture and stir well. Beat egg whites until stiff. Beat cream until stiff. Fold eggs and cream into mixture. Serve with nutmeg on top, if desired.

Hint: Rum is Myers Rum, Original Dark, and 80 proof. Bourbon is Old Grand-Dad Bond, 100 proof.

Yield: 6 servings.

LEMONY-LIGHT COOLER

3 cups dry white wine or white grape juice, chilled
½-¾ cup sugar
½ cup lemon juice from concentrate
1 (32 ounce) bottle club soda, chilled
Strawberries, plum, peach or orange slices or other fresh fruit

In pitcher, combine wine, sugar and lemon juice; stir until sugar dissolves. Just before serving, add club soda and fruit. Serve over ice.

Yield: 2 quarts.

MINT SYRUP CONCENTRATE

2 cups sugar
2½ cups water
1 (6 ounce) can frozen lemon juice
1 (6 ounce) can frozen orange juice
4 large stalks of mint, cut up

Simmer water and sugar for 10 minutes. Add in lemon juice, orange juice and mint. Stir. Cover and let rest for 1 hour. Strain and chill. Fill glasses with crushed ice and pour over one part of this syrup to 2 to 3 parts of water, soda, tonic or gin.

Yield: 32 ounces of concentrate.

SANGRÍA

- ½ gallon Burgundy wine
- 2 green apples, cut into thin slices
- ½ lemon, cut into thin slices
- 1 orange, cut into thin slices
- 1 lime, cut into thin slices
- 2 peaches, cut into slices
- ½ gallon lemon-lime flavored carbonated beverage or club soda
- ½ cup lemonade or limeade, from frozen concentrate

Mix all ingredients together and let is sit for a few hours. It is best if made the day before and refrigerated over night.

Hint: This keeps for a week in the refrigerator and gets a stronger taste with time.

Yield: 3 gallons.

JALAPEÑO MARGARITAS

- 1 pint tequila
- 1 small jalapeño
- 1 large can frozen limeade
- Crushed ice

A couple of days before serving, place 1 sliced and seeded jalapeño in the bottle of tequila. (You can puncture it a few times to make it spicier.) In a pitcher, add 1 can limeade, three cans crushed ice, and ¾ can of tequila. Mix well. Serve in Margarita glasses filled with more crushed ice.

Hint: You need a jalapeño small enough to fit into a bottle. Cutting the jalapeño up will make it especially hot.

Yield: 4 to 6 servings.

SPARKLING STRAWBERRY PUNCH

1 (10 ounce) package frozen (then thawed) strawberries
1½ quarts boiling water
3 family-sized tea bags
½ cup sugar
1 (6 ounce) can lemonade concentrate, thawed and undiluted
2 liters lemon lime carbonated beverage
Fresh mint sprigs, optional

Place strawberries in a blender and process until smooth. Pour boiling water over tea bags and let steep for several minutes. Remove bags. Add sugar and lemonade concentrate to tea. Add in strawberry purée. Chill. Just before serving, add in lemon lime carbonated beverage. Serve on ice. Garnish with mint, if desired.

Yield: 4 quarts.

CRANBERRY GLOGG

⅔ cup cranberry juice
2 tablespoons orange juice
2 teaspoons raisins
¾ teaspoon sugar
1 cinnamon stick
3 whole cloves
Orange wedges

Combine ingredients. Heat, uncovered, in a microwave oven until hot, about 1½ minutes. Can use conventional range, heat until simmering. Garnish with orange wedge.

Yield: 1 serving.

BREAD & BRUNCH COLLECTION

Guanacaste-Nicoya, Costa Rica
Ceremonial Grinding Stone with Jaguar Head, Late Period IV to Early Period V, A.D. 300-700
Volcanic stone, 16½ x 14½ x 37 in.
The Museum of Fine Arts, Houston, museum purchase with funds provided by the Director's Accessions Fund, the Friends of Pre-Columbian Art, and J. Landis Martin in honor of Bill Walker and Matthew R. Simmons at "One Great Night in November, 1990"

Originally serving as a humble grinding stone for maize, chili peppers or other plant foods, the three legged metate in Costa Rica graduated to a specialized form of sculpture and may have assumed a role as insignia for a chief or as a status symbol for a high ranking man. The intricate carving and abundance of undercutting on this example produces the illusion of lace and seemingly defies its origin as a single piece of stone. The jaguar was the largest and the most ferocious animal of the region and was revered as a sun or harvest god.

Bread & Brunch Collection

Applesauce Oat Muffins

Breakfast Meeting Treats

Fran's Coffee Cake

Almond Lime Loaf

Beer Bread

Rick's Waffles

French Coffee Cake

Cheese Bread Rachael

Sweet Potato Biscuits

Potato Rolls

Pumpkin Bread

Strawberry Bread

Rosemary Damper

Zucchini Bread

Cheese Puffs

Spinach Roll

Curried Chicken Tea Sandwiches

Challah French Toast

Baked Apple French Toast

Akuri Spiced Scrambled Eggs

Huevos Rancheros al Pavo

Prysnac

Company's Coming Strata

Quiche without Crust

Spinach and Mushroom Quiche

Swiss Tarts

Honey Puff

APPLESAUCE OAT MUFFINS

¾ cup uncooked oats
¾ cup oat bran
1¼ cups all-purpose flour
2 teaspoons cinnamon
1 teaspoon baking powder
¾ teaspoon baking soda
½ teaspoon salt
1 cup applesauce, unsweetened
½ cup packed brown sugar
⅓ cup vegetable oil
1 egg white
1 teaspoon vanilla
¼ cup chopped nuts
⅓ cup raisins

Preheat oven to 375°. Line muffin pan with 12 paper baking cups. Combine oats, oat bran, flour, cinnamon, baking powder, baking soda, and salt. Add applesauce, brown sugar, oil, egg white and vanilla; mix well. Stir in nuts. Fill muffin cups almost full. Bake 20 to 25 minutes or until golden brown.

Yield: 12 servings.

BREAKFAST MEETING TREATS

½ cup sugar
½ cup softened butter
1-2 teaspoons cinnamon
1 package extra thin white bread
Pecan halves

Mix sugar, butter, and cinnamon. Spread each bread slice with mixture. Cut each slice into quarters. Place pecan half on each quarter. Toast in a 400° oven until bubbly and toasted. Remove and cool. Becomes crispier as cooled.

Note: This is like old-fashioned cinnamon toast. Travels well to meetings and good with coffee.

Yield: 80 pieces.

FRAN'S COFFEE CAKE

1½ cups flour, sift before measuring
3 teaspoons baking powder
½ teaspoon salt
¾ cup sugar
¼ cup butter
1 egg, beaten
½ cup whole milk
1 teaspoon vanilla

Filling and Topping

½ cup brown sugar
2 teaspoons cinnamon
½ cup chopped walnuts
2 tablespoons flour
2 tablespoons melted butter

Mix flour, baking powder, salt and sugar together. Cut in butter with 2 knives until mixture is like fine cornmeal. Blend in well beaten egg mixed with milk. Add vanilla and beat just enough to mix well. Mix filling/topping ingredients together in a separate bowl. Spread ½ of batter in an 8-inch square greased and floured pan and add ½ filling/topping. Spread the rest of the batter in pan and sprinkle on the rest of the topping. Bake in a 375° oven for 25 to 30 minutes.

Yield: 9 servings.

ALMOND-LIME LOAF

3 cups sifted all-purpose flour
1 cup sugar
1 teaspoon baking powder
1 teaspoon salt
¼ teaspoon baking soda
1 cup sliced almonds, divided
2 tablespoons grated lime rind, divided
1 egg
1 cup milk
5 tablespoons butter, melted
3 tablespoons lime juice, divided
2 tablespoons sugar for topping

Grease a 9 X 5 X 3 inch loaf pan. Sift flour, 1 cup sugar, baking powder, salt and baking soda in a large bowl. Stir in ¾ cup of the almonds and 1 tablespoon of the lime rind. Beat egg well with milk in a small bowl. Stir in 4 tablespoons of the melted butter and 2 tablespoons of the lime juice. Add all at once to the flour mixture. Stir until just evenly moist. Spoon into prepared pan. Spread top even. Combine the remaining ¼ cup almonds, 1 tablespoon melted butter, 2 tablespoons sugar and 1 tablespoon lime juice in a cup. Spoon evenly over batter. Bake in a moderate oven (350°) for 1 hour and 10 minutes or until wood pick inserted in center comes out clean. Do not overbake. Cool in pan on wire rack 10 minutes. Loosen around edges with knife and turn out onto rack with almond topping side up. Sprinkle remaining 1 tablespoon lime rind on top (press to adhere). Cool completely. Wrap loaf in waxed paper, foil or transparent wrap. Store overnight to mellow flavors and make slicing easier.

Yield: 12 to 14 servings.

BEER BREAD

3 cups self-rising flour (or 3 cups flour, 1½ teaspoons salt, 4½ teaspoons baking powder)
2 tablespoons sugar
1 (12 ounce) can beer
1 medium onion, chopped OR
1 cup coarsely grated sharp cheddar cheese

Combine all dry ingredients in a large mixing bowl. Add beer and mix well; it will foam. Add onion or cheese or both and work into dough. Put into greased loaf pan. Let rise for 20 minutes. Bake at 375° for 45 minutes. Let stand to cool slightly before inverting onto a platter to slice. Best when served immediately.

Hint: This does not reheat well. It is best with a small group of people who can devour it while it is still hot or warm.

Yield: 6 to 8 servings

RICK'S WAFFLES

2 cups flour
1 teaspoon salt
1 teaspoon baking soda
1 teaspoon baking powder
1 tablespoon sugar
4 eggs
2 cups buttermilk
1 tablespoon vanilla extract
1 cup melted butter

Sift together flour, salt, baking soda, baking powder, and sugar. Beat eggs until light in color. Add dry ingredients and buttermilk alternately to beaten eggs. Add vanilla and melted butter and blend thoroughly.

Yield: 4 servings.

FRENCH COFFEE CAKE

¼ cup butter
1 cup sugar
1 egg
1 teaspoon vanilla
1 cup flour
1 teaspoon baking soda
1 cup sour cream

TOPPING

½ cup chopped pecans
¼ cup brown sugar
1 teaspoon cinnamon
½ cup coconut

Cream the butter and sugar together. Add the egg and vanilla and beat. Add alternately the flour, baking soda and sour cream. Mix the ingredients for the topping in a separate bowl. Put half the topping in the bottom of a greased tube cake pan. Pour the batter on top and sprinkle the remaining topping evenly over the batter. Bake at 350° for approximately 45 minutes. Cool slightly and remove from pan.

Yield: 12 servings.

CHEESE BREAD RACHAEL

Sourdough bread (long large loaf)
1 (8 ounce) package Swiss cheese (sliced)
½ pound butter, softened
2 tablespoons grated onion
2 tablespoons prepared mustard
½ teaspoon Beau Monde seasoning
2 tablespoons lemon juice
1 tablespoon poppy seeds

Preheat oven to 400°. Cut X's in top of bread, almost all the way through to the bottom, but leave 1 inch uncut on each end. Wrap in foil half way up to support the bread (do not cover the top). Place folded cheese in the X cuts, which will form cups. Combine seasoning mix (butter, onion, mustard, Beau Monde, lemon juice, poppy seeds) and spread on the top. Place on a cookie sheet on the bottom rack of the oven. Bake until cheese melts, about 10 to 12 minutes. Serve informally, letting guests pull off chunks of bread from the loaf.

Note: Buy good quality deli cheese and have it sliced. Could also use baby Swiss, Jarlsberg, provolone or mozzarella.

Yield: 4 to 6 servings.

SWEET POTATO BISCUITS

2 cups sifted all-purpose flour
3 teaspoons baking powder
½ teaspoon baking soda
¾ teaspoon salt
Dash of cinnamon
½ cup melted butter
3 tablespoons brown sugar
1 cup boiled, peeled and mashed sweet potatoes
⅔ cup buttermilk

Preheat oven to 450°. Sift flour, baking powder, baking soda, salt and cinnamon and set aside. Using a medium size bowl, beat melted butter into brown sugar and sweet potatoes. Add dry ingredients, stirring in a little at a time, alternating with buttermilk. Mix just well enough to moisten all ingredients. Form into a ball and turn out onto lightly floured board. Lightly pat topside with flour as well since it is a rather sticky batter. Roll out to ½ to ¾-inch thickness with a floured rolling pin. Cut with a floured biscuit cutter. Bake for 20 to 25 minutes.

Yield: 12 to 14 biscuits.

POTATO ROLLS

1 cup hot, mashed potatoes
1½ cups potato water
1 package yeast
½ cup shortening
½ cup sugar
1½ teaspoons salt
1 egg
5 cups flour, divided

Boil potatoes. Reserve liquid. Mash the potatoes. Cool mashed potatoes and potato water to lukewarm. Dissolve yeast in potato water. Melt ½ cup shortening. Combine potatoes, water, and shortening. Add ½ cup sugar, 1½ teaspoons salt, 1 egg and 1 cup flour, mix well and set aside in a warm place for 20 minutes. Add 4 cups flour. Knead well until smooth. Let rise 1 hour. Make into rolls and let rise again until double in size (approximately 15 to 20 minutes). Bake at 400° for 15 minutes.

Yield: 24 rolls.

PUMPKIN BREAD

3½ cups flour
3 cups sugar
1 teaspoon each ginger, cinnamon, nutmeg, and allspice
½ teaspoon salt
2 teaspoons baking soda
2 cups cooked and puréed pumpkin or 1 can prepared pumpkin
1 cup cooking oil
4 eggs
½ cup plus 1 tablespoon water
Nuts, optional

Preheat oven to 350°. Combine flour, sugar, spices, salt and baking soda. Make a well in the center of the mixture and add pumpkin, oil, eggs, and water. Mix well. Add nuts, if desired. Pour into two greased and floured loaf pans. Bake for 1 hour or until bread tests done.

Yield: 8 to 10 slices.

STRAWBERRY BREAD

3 cups flour
1 teaspoon baking soda
1 teaspoon salt
3 teaspoons cinnamon
2 cups sugar
1¼ cups oil
3 eggs, well beaten
2 (10 ounce) packages frozen strawberries, thawed and drained
1¼ cups chopped pecans

Sift dry ingredients into large bowl. Mix oil into eggs and add to flour mixture. Fold in strawberries and pecans and pour into 2 greased 9 X 5 inch loaf pans or 5 small loaf pans. Bake at 350° for 1 hour and 20 minutes or 1 hour for small pans. Cool in pan for 15 minutes.

Hint: Also makes good muffins. Spray muffin tins with vegetable cooking spray and fill ½ to ¾ full. Bake at 350° for approximately 30 to 40 minutes.

Yield: 2 large loaves, 5 small loaves, or 24 muffins.

ROSEMARY DAMPER

3 cups self-rising flour
½ ounce butter or margarine
2 tablespoons fresh chopped rosemary
1 cup grated cheese (cheddar, mozzarella, Swiss, or other)
½ cup milk
¾ cup water

Sift flour and cut in butter. Add the rosemary and ⅔ cup of cheese. Make a well in the center and stir in the milk and enough water to make a soft dough. Knead on a floured surface until smooth. Place on a greased tray and pat into a 5¾-inch round. Using a sharp knife, cut ½-inch deep slices and sprinkle the remaining cheese over the top. Bake in the oven at 350° for 40 minutes.

Yield: 4 to 6 servings.

ZUCCHINI BREAD

3 eggs
2 cups sugar
1 cup oil
1 tablespoon vanilla
2 cups coarsely grated zucchini, unpeeled but scrubbed (2 average sized)
2 cups flour
1 teaspoon cinnamon
2 teaspoons baking powder
1 teaspoon salt
¼ teaspoon baking soda
1 cup chopped pecans
1 (8 ounce) package cream cheese (optional)

Beat eggs until frothy. Beat in sugar. Add oil and vanilla and beat until thick and lemon-colored. Add loosely packed grated zucchini. Sift together dry ingredients and add to egg mixture. Fold in pecans. Pour into 3 greased 8 X 4 inch loaf pans or 5 small loaf pans. Bake at 350° for 1 hour (or 45 minutes for small loaves). Cool in pan at least 10 minutes. Serve plain or with cream cheese.

Yield: 3 medium loaves or 5 small loaves.

CHEESE PUFFS

6 eggs
4 cups packaged biscuit mix
2½ cups milk
3 ounces cream cheese, softened
10 ounces Monterey Jack cheese, grated
6 ounces mild cheddar cheese, grated
1 pound hot sausage, cooked, crumbled, and drained

In a large bowl, beat eggs. Beat in biscuit mix and milk. Mix until smooth. Stir in cheeses and sausage. Pour into 3 quart greased casserole dish. Bake at 350° for 45 minutes.

Yield: 12 servings.

SPINACH ROLL

Dough

1 **teaspoon dry yeast**
1 **cup warm water, divided**
3 **cups flour**
1 **teaspoon salt**
2 **tablespoons olive oil**
1 **tablespoon honey**

Filling

1 **(10 ounce) package chopped frozen spinach, drained**
¼ **cup chopped pepperoni**
1 **egg**
1 **cup shredded mozzarella cheese**
1 **egg white**

Preheat oven to 375°. Sprinkle yeast over ¼ cup warm water to dissolve. Mix flour and salt in a large bowl. Mix ¾ cup water with honey and olive oil. Add yeast/honey/oil mixture to flour and knead several minutes. Cover and let rise in warm place for 2 hours. Roll dough out onto floured board (18 X 12 inch rectangle). Mix filling and spread on dough. Roll up jelly roll fashion. Tuck ends under and put on a greased cookie sheet. Let rise 30 minutes. Brush with egg white. Bake 25 minutes. After cooling, cut into 1-inch slices.

Yield: 12 servings.

CURRIED CHICKEN TEA SANDWICHES

- **½ cup flaked coconut**
- **½ cup almonds, sliced**
- **1 (8 ounce) package cream cheese, softened**
- **2 tablespoons orange marmalade**
- **1½ teaspoons curry powder**
- **3 tablespoons diced green onions**
- **¼ teaspoon salt**
- **2 cups diced cooked chicken**
- **12 (½-inch thick) pumpernickel, wheat, or white bread slices**

Bake coconut and almonds in shallow baking pans at 350°, stirring occasionally, 5 to 10 minutes or until toasted. Stir together cream cheese and next 5 ingredients. Gently stir in chicken. Add coconut and almonds. Spread evenly on bread slices, trim crusts, and cut each slice into 3 strips.

Yield: 36 strips.

CHALLAH FRENCH TOAST

- **1 Challah bread (Traditional Jewish twisted egg bread available in most bakeries)**
- **2 eggs**
- **2 tablespoons milk**
- **2 tablespoon margarine**
- **Powdered sugar, brown sugar, or cinnamon, optional**

Slice Challah bread into ¾ to 1-inch thick slices. Beat eggs with milk and dip both sides of bread into it. Gently fry bread on both sides in margarine. Top with sugar or cinnamon, as desired.

BAKED APPLE FRENCH TOAST

½ cup butter
½ cup brown sugar
1 tablespoon water
3 large green apples (recommend Granny Smith)
8 eggs
3 cups milk
3 tablespoons vanilla
6-12 slices bread (plain white, wheat, French, sourdough, or your favorite)
Cinnamon to taste

Melt butter and add sugar and water. Slice apples (skin on) and simmer in butter mixture for 1-2 minutes. Pour into bottom of greased 9 X 13 inch baking dish and let cool. Beat together eggs, milk and vanilla. Slice bread into halves and layer over apples to cover whole dish. Pour egg mixture over all. Be sure all bread is wet. Sprinkle with cinnamon. Bake at 350° for 40 to 50 minutes or until golden brown and puffy.

Hint: May be made at night and baked in the morning.

Variation: Can substitute other fruit.

Yield: 8 servings.

AKURI SPICED SCRAMBLED EGGS

1 tablespoon oil
1 ounce margarine
3 small onions, finely chopped
5 green chiles, finely chopped
8-10 stems fresh coriander, finely chopped
1 large tomato, skinned, finely chopped
5 eggs
Salt and Pepper to taste

Heat oil and margarine and sauté the onions until golden. Add the remaining ingredients and cook until oil begins to separate and the tomatoes are well done. Set aside. Beat eggs with a fork. Place pan on the heat, add eggs and scramble to desired consistency.

Yield: 4 servings.

HUEVOS RANCHEROS AL PAVO

2 fresh large eggs
1 jar of picante sauce
2 slices baked turkey breast
1 bunch of fresh cilantro

Break two eggs into a small frying pan coated with butter or vegetable cooking spray as desired. Pan should be sizzling hot. After adding eggs, turn fire off and cover pan after adding picante sauce to taste. Allow 5 to 10 minutes for eggs to finish cooking, so that they are "almost blind" but not hard. In the meantime, heat your serving plates and arrange turkey slices on plate, enough turkey to go under the two eggs. Garnish with cilantro.

Yield: 1 serving.

Hint: Serve with sliced tomatoes and avocado. Great way to use leftover holiday turkey.

PRYSNAC

6 large eggs
1 (8 ounce) package cheddar or Old English cheese, diced
6 tablespoons flour
½ cup butter, cut into pieces
24 ounces small curd cottage cheese
1 package chopped broccoli or spinach or fresh equivalents, partially cooked

Combine eggs, diced cheese, flour, butter, and cottage cheese. Mix thoroughly and add spinach and broccoli. Bake 1 hour at 350°, in a buttered casserole dish. Can be prepared ahead.

Yield: 12 to 15 servings.

COMPANY'S COMING STRATA

1 **pound hot or mild breakfast sausage**
6 **eggs**
½ **cup flour**
1 **teaspoon baking powder**
1 **cup milk**
8 **ounces small curd cottage cheese**
3 **ounces cream cheese**
10 **ounces grated Monterey Jack cheese**
6 **ounces grated mild cheddar cheese**
⅛ **teaspoon salt**
6 **tablespoons butter, melted**
8 **slices day old white bread (trim off crusts)**

Cook sausage, drain thoroughly and cool. In a large bowl, beat eggs, flour, baking powder, and milk. Then add remaining ingredients (except bread) and mix together. Place bread in a greased 13 X 9 inch baking dish. Pour entire mixture over bread. Bake 45 minutes at 350° until golden and bubbly. Let stand for a few minutes before cutting into squares.

Hint: Can be made night before. Take out of refrigerator one hour before baking.

Yield: 8 servings.

QUICHE WITHOUT CRUST

3 large eggs
4 ounces lowfat cream cheese
12 ounces lowfat cottage cheese
⅓ cup packaged biscuit mix
½ cup milk
Few drops of hot pepper sauce
¼ teaspoon salt
1 cup grated cheddar cheese
2 tablespoons chopped green onion
1 pound spinach, sautéed in 1 tablespoon of butter or margarine
2 tablespoons chopped dried tomato
½ cup chopped chicken, ham or turkey, optional
½ cup chopped mushrooms, optional
1 cup grated Swiss cheese, optional

Place eggs, cream cheese, cottage cheese, biscuit mix, and milk in blender. Add seasoning and blend until almost smooth. Pour into quiche dish. Add cheese, onions and spinach. (Add other optional ingredients, if desired.) Bake in a 9 inch pie pan 30 to 40 minutes at 350° until filling is set.

Hint: Good served as an appetizer for brunch or lunch or as a light supper. Leftovers are good heated or cold. Can be served on lettuce greens or with fruit. Recipe can be tripled and baked in a 3 quart casserole and cut into squares for 10 to 12 people.

Yield: 6 servings.

SPINACH AND MUSHROOM QUICHE

1 (9-inch) pie crust
1 onion, diced
1 package of chopped, frozen spinach
1 (8 ounce) package of mushrooms, sliced
3 eggs, beaten
1 cup shredded cheese (cheddar, mozzarella, Swiss, or a combination)
⅔ cup milk
Salt and pepper to taste

Bake the pie crust at 375° for 8 to 10 minutes until slightly golden and remove from oven. Sauté the onion until translucent. Add mushrooms and spinach and cook for 10 minutes. Drain. Add remaining ingredients. Pour mixture into pie crust and bake for an additional 20 to 25 minutes.

Yield: 6 servings.

SWISS TARTS

6 unbaked, 4-inch tart shells
6 slices bacon
2 tablespoons reserved bacon fat
2 eggs, slightly beaten
¾ cup sour cream
½ teaspoon salt
1 cup chopped onion
2½ cups (12 ounces) Swiss cheese, grated
Dash pepper

Preheat oven to 375°. Bake tarts 25 to 30 minutes. Fry bacon until crisp; drain and reserve bacon fat. Cook onion in bacon fat until tender. Combine eggs, sour cream, salt, onion, cheese, crumbled bacon and dash of pepper. Pour into tart shells and bake on cookie sheet.

Hint: If using frozen tart shells, thaw, then bake at 375° approximately 5 minutes. Cool before filling.

Yield: 6 servings.

HONEY PUFF

6 eggs
1 cup flour
1 cup milk
3 tablespoons honey
½ teaspoon salt
½ teaspoon baking powder
1 teaspoon vanilla
3 ounces cream cheese
2-4 tablespoons butter
Powdered sugar

Preheat oven to 375°. Put all ingredients in blender. Once the oven is heated to 375°, put an ovenproof metal skillet in the oven with the butter. Immediately blend the batter for 1 to 2 minutes. Once the butter sizzles, pour the batter into the pan. Close the oven and let bake for 25 minutes or until inserted knife in center comes out clean. Sprinkle with powdered sugar.

Hint: Great with fruit and sausage.

Yield: 8 servings.

SOUP, SALAD & SAUCE COLLECTION

Worcester Porcelain Manufactory, English, established 1751
Covered Sauce Tureen and Ladle, 1784-85
Soft-paste porcelain, 4¾ x 6⅝ x 4¼ in. (covered tureen), 6½ x 2 x 1⅛ in. (ladle)
The Museum of Fine Arts, Houston, the Rienzi Collection, museum purchase with funds provided by Mr. & Mrs. Harris Masterson III

This excellent piece of Worcester porcelain bears the Arms of Bostock with Rich in Pretence. Decorated with garlands of flowers, succulent fruit, a black steed and a shield, this piece pays tribute to the tradition of heraldry in England. The wide range of colors used and the gold gilt enhance the beauty of the fluted shape. Not as dense as Chinese porcelain, Worcester tableware is smooth, thin and feels warm to the touch.

Soup, Salad & Sauce Collection

Aimee's Bombay Chiller
Chilled Cucumber Soup
Cajun Veggie Chili
Creamy Artichoke Soup
Spiced Broth
Portuguese Kale Soup
Portuguese Soup
Cowboy Cheddar Soup
Mardi Gras Soup
Amy's Brie Soup
Frosted Beet Soup
Gazpacho
Gazpacho with Sour Cream
Calabacitas (Cream of Squash Soup)
Curried Pumpkin Soup
Chicken Enchilada Soup
Taos Society Soup (Roasted Red Pepper Soup)
Creole Corn Chowder Soup
Valerie's Tortilla Soup
Shrimp Salad
Tex-Mex Marinated Salad
Butch's Wild West Tex-Mex Salad
Oriental Salad
Diego Rivera Salad
Gougère with Gruyère Salad
Spinach Salad
Christmas Salad
Tabbouleh
Greek Salad
Orzo Salad
Nutty Wild Rice Salad
Black Bean, Orzo and Tomato Salad
Chicken Salad
Sybil's Chicken Salad
Hot Chicken Salad
Black-Eyed Pea Salad
Barbara Lea's Chicken Salad
White Bean Tuna Salad
Marian's Luncheon Salad
Curried Shrimp Salad
Chicken and Pecan Rice Salad
Corn Salad
Fumi Salad
Broccoli Cole Slaw
Confetti Cole Slaw
Potato Salad Diane
Dilled Potato Salad
Roasted Potato Salad
Virginia's Tomato Aspic
Fancy Mustard
Pepper Jelly
Brandied Cranberry Sauce
Frosted Raspberry Salad
Fresh Cranberry Relish
Cranberry Salad
Cranberry Chutney
Cocktail Sauce
Basil Pesto
French Dressing
Creamy Basil Dressing
Balsamic Dressing
Mango Chutney
Jezebel Sauce
Meat Marinade I
Meat Marinade II
Mayonnaise from Rienzi
Marianna's Mustard Sauce

AIMEE'S BOMBAY CHILLER

1 (10½ ounce) can cream of chicken soup (can use reduced fat)
1 soup can of milk (can use low fat)
1 tablespoon curry powder
3 tablespoons fresh lemon juice
Chutney
Sliced or chopped green apples
Pistachio nuts, chopped coarsely
Coconut flakes

Mix first 4 ingredients in blender. Chill until icy cold. Makes 2½ cups. When serving, add chutney, tart apples, and pistachios to taste. Top with coconut.

Yield: 5 servings.

CHILLED CUCUMBER SOUP

1 cup condensed chicken broth
2 tablespoons lemon juice
¼ cup finely chopped onion
1 teaspoon salt
½ teaspoon dried dill weed, crushed
Dash of garlic powder
1 teaspoon grated lemon rind
1 cup sour cream
1 cup plain yogurt
2 medium cucumbers, peeled, chopped and drained

Combine and blend broth, lemon juice, onion, salt, dill weed, garlic powder and lemon rind until smooth. Add in sour cream and yogurt, mix until just blended. Stir in cucumber. Serve chilled.

Yield: 4 servings.

CAJUN VEGGIE CHILI

2 tablespoons olive oil
1 large bunch fresh spinach (stems removed), washed well and coarsely chopped
Salt and freshly ground black pepper to taste
2 tablespoons lemon juice
Cooked white rice for serving
½ cup nonfat plain yogurt
4 green onions, chopped
1 large onion, peeled and diced ¼-inch
1 green bell pepper, cored, seeded and diced ¼-inch
1 red bell pepper, cored, seeded and diced ¼-inch
1 tablespoon minced garlic
2½ tablespoons chili powder
1 tablespoon ground marjoram
1 (28 ounce) can peeled plum tomatoes
2 teaspoons dried thyme
1 (8 ounce) can garbanzo beans
1 (8 ounce) can black beans
1 cup corn (can use canned)
Sausage, optional

Place the oil, onion and peppers in a large, heavy pot over low heat. Cook, stirring occasionally, for 10 to 12 minutes or until the vegetables are very soft. Add garlic and cook for 2 minutes over low heat to prevent burning. Add chili powder and marjoram. Cook, stirring, for 1 minute. Add tomatoes and thyme. Simmer over medium heat for 10 minutes. Add the garbanzo beans, black beans, and corn. Add in sausage, if desired. Cook, stirring occasionally, 10 minutes longer. Remove from heat. Add the spinach and stir until it is well combined and wilted. Season generously with salt and pepper and stir in the lemon juice. Serve over white rice. Garnish with a dollop of yogurt and green onions.

Variation: If using sausage, brown with oil, onion and peppers.

Yield: 6 to 8 servings.

CREAMY ARTICHOKE SOUP

2 cups light cream
2 egg yolks
4 large or 6 small (or 1 can, not marinated) artichoke hearts, drained and chopped
6 tablespoons butter
½ cup onion, chopped
½ cup celery, chopped
6 tablespoons flour
6 cups clear chicken broth
¼ cup lemon juice
1 bay leaf
1 teaspoon salt (omit if using bouillon or canned broth)
¼ teaspoon pepper
¼ teaspoon thyme

Slightly beat egg yolks in cream and set aside. Sauté onion and celery until soft, but not browned. Stir in flour. Cook, stirring constantly, for 1 minute. Add chicken stock and lemon juice until blended. Add seasonings and chopped artichoke hearts. Cover and simmer until slightly thickened, about 20 minutes. Purée in blender a cup at a time. Return to skillet. Heat to boil. Remove from heat and add cream with egg yolks.

Hint: To reheat, pour into heavy skillet or into a double boiler and warm on low heat. Do not boil.

Yield: 8 servings.

SPICED BROTH

2 cups chicken broth
½ cup clam juice
¼ cup sherry
1 green onion bottom, thinly sliced, crossways
Freshly ground pepper to taste

Combine all ingredients in a small saucepan. Heat to blend flavors.

Hint: This is great on a cold day to warm you up quickly from the inside. Travels well in a thermos.

Yield: 2 servings.

PORTUGUESE KALE SOUP

2 tablespoons oil
½ pound chorizo sausage
1 large onion, coarsely chopped
1 teaspoon cumin
1 teaspoon thyme
½ pound new potatoes, small dice
1 (14 ounce) can chopped tomatoes
1 (10 ounce) can spicy tomatoes and chiles
1 (15 ounce) can red kidney beans
2 cups chicken broth
1 bunch kale

Heat oil, sauté sausage and onions until lightly browned. Add cumin and thyme. Microwave potatoes for 5 minutes. Add tomatoes, tomatoes and chiles, kidney beans, sausage mixture and chicken broth. Cook for 30 minutes. Wash kale and cut out the tough stems, chop into large pieces. Add to the soup mixture. Cook 5 minutes more or until kale is wilted.

Yield: 8 servings.

PORTUGUESE SOUP

6 cups chicken stock or broth
1 pound smoked kielbasa sausage, diced
1 pound small potatoes, diced and peeled
1 (15 ounce) can kidney beans
1 (15 ounce) can diced tomatoes
½ (medium) head of green cabbage, coarsely chopped
1 medium onion, chopped
8 large carrots, diced
1 green pepper, diced
3 large cloves garlic, minced
Salt and pepper to taste

Combine all ingredients in large pot. Bring to a boil, stirring occasionally. Reduce heat and simmer approximately 2 hours, stirring occasionally. Season with salt and pepper to taste.

Yield: 8 servings.

COWBOY CHEDDAR SOUP

2 tablespoons butter
3 tablespoons flour
4 cups milk
¾ teaspoon salt
½ teaspoon dry mustard
¼ teaspoon cayenne pepper
1 (10 ounce) package broccoli, thawed and drained
½ cup finely chopped red bell pepper
6 ounces sharp cheddar cheese, shredded
2 tablespoons chopped chives or green onion tops

Melt butter in skillet. Add flour and cook, stirring constantly for about 30 seconds. Add milk, salt, dry mustard and cayenne. Stir constantly on low heat until thickened. Add broccoli and red bell pepper. Reduce heat and simmer 5 minutes, uncovered, stirring occasionally. Add cheese and stir until cheese melts. Do not let it boil. Top with chives and serve.

Yield: 4 servings.

MARDI GRAS SOUP

- 2 green onions, sliced
- 5 leeks, white and pale green portions, thinly sliced
- 2 tablespoons unsalted butter
- 4 medium potatoes, peeled and thinly sliced
- ¼ cup dry white wine
- 5 cups chicken broth
- 1 cup half and half
- Dash salt
- Dash white pepper
- Cucumber, sliced for garnish
- Violets for garnish

In a large saucepan, sauté green onions and leeks in the butter over low heat for 10 minutes. Add potatoes, wine and broth. Bring to a boil. Reduce to simmer. Cover and cook 25 minutes. Process in small batches in a food processor until smooth. Add half-and-half. Salt and pepper to taste and mix well. Chill. Serve cold in individual soup bowls. Garnish with various cucumber shapes. Float a violet on each serving.

Yield: 8 servings.

AMY'S BRIE SOUP

- ¾ cup onion, chopped
- ½ cup celery, chopped
- 4 tablespoons butter
- 2 tablespoons flour
- 1 pint half and half
- 16 ounces (2 cups) chicken broth
- ½ pound Brie cheese, rind removed
- 1 cup chopped green chiles

Sauté onion and celery in butter. When soft, stir in flour. Add half and half, stirring well to make a roux. Add broth, stir well and simmer. When hot, add Brie and stir to melt. Add green chiles. Serve hot.

Yield: 4 servings.

FROSTED BEET SOUP

2 cups beef broth
1 medium cucumber, peeled, seeded and chopped
1 large onion, sliced
½ bay leaf
¼ teaspoon dried basil
1 (16 ounce) can sliced beets, undrained
1 tablespoon fresh lemon juice
½ teaspoon granulated sugar
½ cup yogurt
Garlic powder to taste
Sliced green onions or chopped chives (garnish)

In a 3 quart saucepan, put beef broth, cucumber, onion, bay leaf and basil. Bring to a boil, lower heat and cook for 10 minutes until vegetables are tender. Remove bay leaf, add beets and beet liquid, lemon juice and garlic powder. Purée in small batches in blender. Before serving, stir in ½ cup yogurt and garnish with green onions or chives.

Yield: 6 to 8 servings.

GAZPACHO

1½ cups tomato juice
1 chicken bouillon cube or 1 teaspoon instant chicken bouillon
1 tomato, chopped
¼ cup chopped cucumber, skin on
2 tablespoons chopped green pepper
2 tablespoons chopped onion
2 tablespoons white wine vinegar
1 tablespoon olive oil
½ teaspoon salt
½ teaspoon white wine Worcestershire sauce
3 drops red pepper sauce

Heat tomato juice to boiling. Add bouillon cubes; stir until dissolved. Stir in remaining ingredients. Chill several hours.

Yield: 2 servings.

GAZPACHO WITH SOUR CREAM

2-3 cucumbers, chopped
1 medium to large onion, chopped
1 avocado, chopped (optional)
2-3 tomatoes, chopped
1 bell pepper, chopped
6 tablespoons vegetable oil
4 tablespoons white wine vinegar
8 cups tomato juice
Juice of 4 limes
3-4 dashes hot pepper sauce
1 teaspoon salt
1 container sour cream
Croutons

Mix all ingredients (except sour cream and croutons) and refrigerate. Best made the night before you want to serve it. Serve topped with a dollop of sour cream and croutons.

Yield: 8 to 10 servings.

CALABACITAS (CREAM OF SQUASH SOUP)

¼ cup butter, melted
2 tablespoons vegetable oil
1 large onion, minced
6-7 cloves garlic, minced
¼ teaspoon basil
3 pounds squash (12 to 13 small green zucchini) thinly sliced
4 cups chicken broth
8-12 ounces whipping cream
1½ teaspoons salt
½ teaspoon white pepper or finely ground black pepper

Melt butter and oil in Dutch oven. Sauté onion and garlic until tender. Add basil. Stir in squash and chicken broth. Cover and simmer until tender (30 to 35 minutes). Purée squash mixture in batches until smooth. Add cream, salt and pepper. Serve hot or cold.

Yield: 11 to 12 cups.

CURRIED PUMPKIN SOUP

1 large onion, chopped
½ cup butter
½ cup flour
2 quarts chicken stock
1-4 teaspoons curry, to taste
2 cups canned pumpkin
2 teaspoons honey
Salt and pepper, to taste
1 cup light cream
1 pound sliced mushrooms, optional
Sour cream and chives or parsley for garnish, optional

Sauté onions in butter. Add flour and cook 2 to 4 minutes, stirring gently. Do not brown. Add chicken stock and cook until slightly thickened. Add pumpkin, onion, honey and seasonings. Cook for 20 minutes. Add cream and mushrooms, if desired. Heat well. To serve, garnish with a dollop of sour cream and top with chives or parsley, if desired.

Yield: 6 to 8 servings.

CHICKEN ENCHILADA SOUP

1½ cups chicken stock
12 corn tortillas, cut into strips
1 (10 ounce) can enchilada sauce with green chiles
1 (10 ounce) can medium to hot enchilada sauce
1 teaspoon ground cumin
4 boneless, skinless chicken breast halves, grilled and sliced
1 cup half and half
1 medium tomato, diced
1 small jalapeño, seeded and minced
1 cup finely grated cheddar cheese
Crisp tortilla chips

Combine chicken stock and tortilla strips in a large pot. Cook over medium heat until strips begin to soften and broth thickens somewhat. Add enchilada sauces and cumin. Add chicken and half-and-half. Heat through. Divide among 4 bowls and garnish with diced tomatoes, jalapeños, and cheese. Serve with tortilla chips.

Yield: 4 servings.

TAOS SOCIETY SOUP (ROASTED RED PEPPER SOUP)

5 red bell peppers
2 tablespoons butter
2 cups chopped onion
1-2 tablespoons crushed garlic
1 teaspoon salt
Black pepper
½ teaspoon cumin
1 tablespoon white flour
½ cup chicken stock
2½ cups milk, room temperature
Sour cream, thinned
Cilantro, chopped

Place peppers on oiled tray and put in a 350° oven for approximately 45 minutes or until the skin puckers and burns. Turn the peppers every 15 minutes so that peppers blister evenly. Place peppers in paper bag for about 10 minutes. Once cooled, skin should come off easily. Without putting pepper under water (water will remove smoky flavor), remove skin, seeds and core and slice. Melt butter in a kettle or soup pot. Add onions and garlic and cook slowly. Add salt, pepper and cumin. Cook about 10 minutes, until onions are soft. Add bell peppers, stir and cover. Cook over low heat about 15 minutes, stirring every few minutes. Sprinkle in flour and stir, continue cooking, about 5 minutes. Add stock, stir and cook about 5 minutes. Remove from heat. Using a blender, purée the mixture in batches, with milk. Put the puréed soup in a soup pot or kettle and heat gently. Take several tablespoons of sour cream and thin by whisking it with a whisk or fork. When ready to serve, pour soup into bowls and using fork, drizzle in the sour cream. Top with chopped cilantro and serve.

Yield: 6 servings.

CREOLE CORN CHOWDER SOUP

½ pound bacon, diced
1 medium bell pepper, chopped
1 small yellow onion, chopped
1 small jar pimentos
1 clove garlic, minced
1 (10 ounce) can diced tomatoes
2 (15 ounce) cans whole kernel corn, drained
2 cups tomato juice
½ teaspoon thyme
½ teaspoon oregano
½ teaspoon basil
½ teaspoon red pepper
1½ cups milk
1 cup heavy cream

Sauté bacon until fat rendered, remove bacon and dice (reserve fat). Add pepper, onion, pimentos, and garlic and sauté. Add rest of ingredients (except milk and cream). Bring to a boil, reduce heat and simmer 20 minutes. Add milk and cream and simmer 20 more minutes. Adjust seasoning to taste.

Hint: If spicier soup desired, use canned tomatoes with chiles. Can be made day ahead, adding milk and cream and simmering the last 20 minutes before serving.

Yield: 8 to 10 servings.

VALERIE'S TORTILLA SOUP

2 chicken breasts
½ cup Monterey Jack cheese
3-4 corn tortillas
1 carrot, finely chopped
1 small yellow onion, chopped
2 garlic cloves, minced
2 tablespoons oil
1 (10 ounce) can diced tomatoes
2 cups chicken broth
1 tablespoon tomato paste
3-4 sprigs epazote
1 teaspoon cumin
1 teaspoon chili powder
Salt and pepper to taste
1 avocado, chopped
Juice of 1 lime
Sliced lime garnish

Poach chicken breasts, cool, tear into strips. Set aside. Grate cheese. Set aside. Cut tortillas into strips, fry and set aside. Sauté carrot, onion and garlic until just tender. Add tomatoes, broth, tomato paste, epazote and spices. Simmer about 45 minutes. When serving, place chicken, tortillas and cheese in each bowl. Ladle soup over these ingredients. Top each with lime juice and chopped avocado. Place thin lime slice on top. Serve hot.

Yield: 2 Servings.

SHRIMP SALAD

1-2 pounds small shrimp, boiled and peeled
1 cup celery, coarsely chopped
2 hard-cooked eggs, finely chopped
½ cup chopped Bermuda onion or other mild onion
1 small jar capers
½ teaspoon Worcestershire sauce
2 tablespoons mayonnaise
Salt and pepper to taste
Hot sauce to taste

Combine all ingredients. Serve on lettuce, avocado halves, or tomatoes.

Yield: 8 servings.

TEX-MEX MARINATED SALAD

1 (16 ounce) can red kidney beans, drained and rinsed
1 cup chopped green bell pepper
1 cup chopped yellow bell pepper
1 tablespoon minced jalapeño
¾ cup chopped onion
⅓ cup white wine vinegar
2 tablespoons vegetable oil
3 tablespoons chopped cilantro
1 teaspoon chili powder

Combine first five ingredients in bowl and mix well. In separate bowl, mix vinegar, oil, cilantro, and chili powder. Stir well, pour over beans and vegetables, toss to coat. Cover and refrigerate 8 hours or overnight, stirring occasionally. Toss before serving.

Yield: 8 servings.

BUTCH'S WILD WEST TEX-MEX SALAD

Salad

3 (15½ ounce to 19 ounce) cans black beans, rinsed and drained
4 (15½ ounce to 19 ounce) cans whole kernel corn, drained
3 cups cooked white rice
¾ cup finely chopped red onion
½ cup finely chopped green onion, including tops
½ cup chopped fresh cilantro
2 cups coarsely chopped tomatoes
Cilantro sprigs and lime wedges for garnish

Dressing

1 cup olive oil and vinegar salad dressing
¾ cup red wine vinegar
3 tablespoons chipotle peppers in adobe sauce, chopped
Juice of 1 large lime (about 2 tablespoons)
1 tablespoon ground cumin
2 teaspoons salt

Prepare dressing by whisking all ingredients together. Mix beans, corn, rice, red and green onions, and ½ cup cilantro in a large bowl. Add dressing mixture and toss. Marinate salad, covered, in refrigerator at least 1 hour or up to 24 hours. Before serving, add tomato. Garnish with cilantro and lime wedges.

Hint: Chipotle peppers in adobo sauce are available in Hispanic markets.

Yield: 6 servings.

ORIENTAL SALAD

Salad

2 heads romaine lettuce, washed and drained
2 small cans Mandarin oranges
½ pound bacon, fried crisp
1 package sliced almonds
Red onion rings, cut into rings

Dressing

⅓ cup sugar
2½ tablespoons vinegar
½ tablespoon lemon juice
2 tablespoons honey
½ teaspoon grated onion
½ teaspoon dry mustard
½ teaspoon paprika
½ teaspoon celery seed
⅛ teaspoon salt
½ cup salad oil

Drain oranges, crumble bacon. Brown almonds in the bacon drippings. Drain on paper towels. Tear lettuce into bite sized pieces. Add onion. When ready to serve, toss all the ingredients. Make the salad dressing by combining all ingredients except the salad oil and heat just until sugar is dissolved, stirring constantly. After cooling dressing mixture, add oil. Place salad dressing in a mixing jar. Shake well and add to salad just before serving.

Yield: 6 servings.

DIEGO RIVERA SALAD

SALAD

1 head lettuce or 4 to 6 cups mixed greens (romaine, leaf lettuce, and spinach) torn into bite-size pieces
1 grapefruit, peeled and sectioned, each section cut into thirds
1 avocado, cubed
2-3 tablespoons pumpkin seeds
¼ cup pomegranate seeds

DRESSING

1 cup olive oil and vinegar salad dressing
1-2 tablespoons honey, to taste

In a large bowl, combine lettuce, grapefruit sections, avocado, pumpkin seeds, and pomegranate seeds. Add honey to dressing and dress salad lightly.

Yield: 6 to 8 servings.

GOUGÈRE WITH GRUYÈRE SALAD

4 tablespoons butter
½ cup water
½ cup flour
2 eggs, beaten lightly
3 ounces grated Gruyère
4 ounces baby salad greens sprinkled with olive oil and lemon juice
2 ounces Gruyère, shaved into thin curls

Put the butter, water, and a pinch of salt in a small pan, heat gently to melt the butter, then bring to a boil. Add the flour all at once, then lower the heat and stir until you have a smooth mixture. Take the pan off the heat and beat in the eggs, a quarter at a time, until the mixture becomes smooth and glossy. Stir in two thirds of the grated Gruyère and spoon the mixture on to a baking sheet lined with baking parchment to form a ring about 10 inches in diameter. Sprinkle with the remaining grated Gruyère and bake for about 20 minutes at 425°, until puffed and golden. Prepare the salad and pile the salad in the center of the gougère ring and cover with curls of Gruyère.

Yield: 6 servings.

SPINACH SALAD

Salad

2 bags spinach
1 can water chestnuts, drained
2 hard-cooked eggs
Bacon, fried

Dressing

¾ cup sugar
¼ cup red wine vinegar
1 cup salad oil
2 tablespoons Worcestershire sauce
⅓ cup ketchup
1 medium onion, sliced into strips

Wash spinach and dry thoroughly. Add sliced water chestnuts. Add sliced hard-cooked eggs. Add bacon (as much as you like) cut into small pieces. Mix dressing ingredients as listed. Toss with salad before serving.

Yield: 6 servings.

CHRISTMAS SALAD

2 large heads romaine lettuce, cut up
8 ounces dried cranberries
8 ounces slivered almonds, toasted
4 ounces Gorgonzola cheese, crumbled
2 pounds tangerines, peeled and sectioned
⅔ bottle champagne vinaigrette

All ingredients can be prepared in advance. Toss everything together right before serving.

Yield: 20 servings.

TABBOULEH

½ cup cracked wheat (bulghur wheat)
2 cups finely minced parsley
2 cups finely chopped tomatoes
1 cup finely chopped cucumber
1 cup finely chopped green onion
½ cup finely chopped mint leaves
¾ cup olive oil
¼ cup lemon juice
1 head lettuce, leaves separated

Clean bulghur and wash 3 to 4 times. Drain and put aside. Mix other ingredients. Add bulghur. Mix. Serve on lettuce leaves.

Yield: 6 to 8 servings.

GREEK SALAD

Salad

9 cups salad greens (do not use iceberg lettuce)
1 cup ripe kalamata olives
3 plum tomatoes, cut into wedges
1 small red onion, thinly sliced
½ medium cucumber, cut into wedges
3 small cooked beets, quartered
½ bell pepper, cut into 1-inch pieces
8 ounces feta cheese, sliced or crumbled
Fresh Greek Dressing (recipe follows)

Dressing

½ cup olive oil
Juice of 1 lemon (¼ cup)
1 clove garlic, minced or 2 cloves pressed
1 teaspoon dried oregano leaves
Salt and freshly ground black pepper to taste

Mix all the dressing ingredients together. Toss the salad ingredients. Top with feta cheese and serve with dressing.

Yield: 6 servings.

ORZO SALAD

1 pound orzo, boiled and drained
½ cup lemon juice
⅔ cup olive oil
½ cup green onion, chopped
⅓ cup parsley, chopped
½ pound feta cheese, crumbled

Cook pasta and drain. Mix lemon juice and olive oil, set aside. Add onions, parsley, and feta cheese to pasta and toss. Add olive oil and lemon juice mixture last and mix well. Refrigerate for 2 hours before serving.

Yield: 8 servings.

NUTTY WILD RICE SALAD

Salad

½ cup wild rice
2 cups canned beef broth, undiluted
1 cup frozen peas, thawed
2 stalks celery, thinly sliced
4 green onions, sliced
¼ cup slivered almonds, toasted

Dressing

2 tablespoons red wine vinegar
1 tablespoon soy sauce
1 teaspoon sugar
¼ cup canola oil
2 teaspoons sesame oil

In medium saucepan, combine rice with enough cold water to cover an inch above rice. Heat to boiling. Drain water from rice and add broth. Simmer covered until liquid is absorbed, about 1 hour. Set aside. Mix dressing ingredients together and set aside. While rice is still warm, toss with dressing; cool. In medium bowl, combine rice with peas, celery, green onions and almonds. Toss well. Refrigerate.

Yield: 6 servings.

BLACK BEAN, ORZO AND TOMATO SALAD

- **1 cup orzo pasta**
- **1½ teaspoons salt, divided**
- **2 (19 ounce) cans black beans, rinsed, drained and dried**
- **1½ cups seeded, diced tomatoes**
- **½ cup chopped sweet red onion**
- **1½ tablespoons Dijon mustard**
- **3 tablespoons red wine vinegar**
- **1 tablespoon minced garlic**
- **¼ teaspoon crushed red pepper flakes**
- **6 tablespoons olive oil**
- **2 tablespoons chopped parsley**
- **3 tablespoons chopped basil**

Bring 2 quarts water to boil and add orzo and 1 teaspoon salt. Cook 8 to 10 minutes. Drain well and pat dry. Place orzo in bowl and add beans, tomatoes, and onion. Mix well. In another bowl, whisk together mustard, vinegar, garlic, pepper flakes and ½ teaspoon salt. Gradually whisk in olive oil. Pour dressing over salad and toss. Add more salt and red pepper, if needed. Refrigerate. Add parsley and basil before serving.

Yield: 6 servings.

CHICKEN SALAD

- **2 cups diced, cooked chicken**
- **½ cup chopped celery**
- **¼ cup chopped onion**
- **¼ cup chopped green pepper**
- **¼ cup sweet relish**
- **1 tablespoon parsley flakes**
- **1 cup white seedless grapes**
- **1 carrot, cut into strips (garnish)**

Mix ingredients in the order listed. Serve on a bed of lettuce. Garnish with carrot strips.

Yield: 4 to 6 servings.

SYBIL'S CHICKEN SALAD

4 cups cooked chicken breast, cut into bite sized pieces
1½ cups celery, cut diagonally into ¼ to ½-inch slices (reserve tops)
2 tablespoons chopped parsley
10-12 black peppercorns
1 cup mayonnaise
1 cup sour cream
1½ teaspoons salt
½ teaspoon pepper
2 tablespoons lemon juice
½ cup toasted sliced almonds

Cook chicken by placing approximately 6 chicken breasts in a pot and cover with water. Add celery tops with leaves, 3 to 4 sprigs parsley, and 10 to 12 peppercorns. Poach until tender. Remove from broth and cool. Mix together chicken, sliced celery, and parsley. Mix together mayonnaise, sour cream, salt, pepper and lemon juice. Add to chicken mixture. Chill well before serving, preferably overnight. When ready to serve, sprinkle toasted almonds over top of salad.

Yield: 6 servings.

HOT CHICKEN SALAD

1 cup mayonnaise
2 teaspoons lemon juice
1 teaspoon grated lemon peel
2 teaspoons grated onion
½ teaspoon salt
2½ cups cooked, diced chicken breasts
1 cup chopped celery
1 cup slivered toasted almonds
½ cup grated sharp cheddar cheese
1 cup browned bread crumbs

Blend mayonnaise with lemon peel, lemon juice, onion and salt. Mix lightly with chicken, celery and almonds. Spoon into 1½ quart casserole. Top with a sprinkling of cheese and bread crumbs. Bake at 400° for 15 minutes or until piping hot.

Hint: You can make with shrimp, turkey, or crabmeat

Yield: 4 to 6 servings.

BLACK-EYED PEA SALAD

4 ribs celery, chopped
1 red bell pepper, chopped
4 green onions, chopped
2 (15½ ounce) cans black-eyed peas, drained and rinsed
½ cup minced fresh cilantro
½ cup Italian dressing (may use fat-free)
2 tablespoons Dijon mustard
Leaf lettuce, optional

Combine chopped vegetables, black-eyed peas, and next three ingredients in a large glass bowl. Cover and chill for at least 4 hours (or overnight). Serve on a bed of lettuce, if desired.

Variation: Add 2 cups of chicken for Chicken and Black-Eyed Pea Salad.

Yield: 8 servings.

BARBARA LEA'S CHICKEN SALAD

6 cups chopped cooked chicken
1½ cups sliced celery
1 (8 ounce) can pineapple tidbits, drained
1¼ cups reduced fat mayonnaise
2½ tablespoons dry white wine
¾ teaspoon salt
¾ teaspoon curry powder
Lettuce
Apples, sliced
Cantaloupe, sliced
Strawberries, sliced
Blackberries
Grapes
¼ cup toasted walnuts, pecans or almonds

Combine chicken, celery, and pineapple. Set aside. In a separate bowl, combine mayonnaise, white wine, salt, and curry powder. Add to chicken mixture. Cover and chill 1 to 2 hours. Arrange on a plate with lettuce and fruit. Sprinkle with nuts.

Yield: 8 to 10 servings.

WHITE BEAN TUNA SALAD

4 cups cooked white beans, rinsed and chilled (may use canned)
¼ cup olive oil
½ teaspoon salt
½ teaspoon cracked pepper
1 tablespoon lemon juice
1-2 (7 ounce) cans Italian tuna in olive oil, drained
2 finely chopped red onions
2 tablespoons chopped parsley

Combine oil, lemon juice, salt and pepper. Pour over beans. Add tuna, onions and parsley. Mix well.

Yield: 4 servings.

MARIAN'S LUNCHEON SALAD

Dressing

½ **cup oil**
¼ **cup lemon juice**
1 teaspoon sugar
½ **teaspoon salt**
¼ **teaspoon pepper**
⅛ **teaspoon tarragon leaves**

Salad

3 cups cubed cooked chicken
2 cups cooked wild rice
¼ **cup chopped bell pepper**
¼ **cup sliced green onion**
½ **cup almond slivers**
2 cups pineapple chunks (drained)

Combine dressing, set aside. Combine chicken, rice, bell pepper, onion, and almonds. Mix in dressing and pineapple just before serving.

Yield: 8 servings.

CURRIED SHRIMP SALAD

1 pound cooked and shelled shrimp
1 cup diced or sliced celery
3 green onions, chopped (optional)
½ **cup mayonnaise**
½ **cup sour cream**
Juice of 1 lemon
1-1½ teaspoon curry powder
½ **teaspoon salt**

Mix all of the ingredients together, except the shrimp. Add shrimp and mix to coat evenly.

Yield: 6 servings.

CHICKEN AND PECAN RICE SALAD

Salad

4 cups chicken stock
1 package "Wild Blend" rice
4 boneless, skinless chicken breasts, poached
1 cup chopped pecans
3 green onions, sliced
1 cup chopped celery
½ cup raisins

Vinaigrette

¼ cup rice vinegar
¼ cup orange juice
2 tablespoons Dijon mustard
2 tablespoons mango chutney
½ teaspoon salt
¼ teaspoon white pepper
½ cup vegetable oil

Cook rice according to directions using chicken stock instead of water. Remove from heat. Cool to room temperature. Combine rice, chicken, pecans, green onions, raisins, and celery in a large bowl. In separate bowl, whisk oil into vinegar, orange juice, mustard, chutney, salt, and pepper until slightly thickened and thoroughly combined. Pour vinaigrette over rice and chicken mixture. Toss gently. Marinate at least 4 hours, or overnight, in the refrigerator.

Yield: 8 servings.

CORN SALAD

1 small jar chopped pimentos
1 (11 ounce) can white shoepeg corn, drained
1 (15 ounce) can very small English peas, drained
½ cup finely chopped celery
½ cup finely chopped onion
6 tablespoons mayonnaise

Mix all ingredients.

Variation: You can add chopped chicken, tuna, or cubed cheese.

Yield: 8 servings.

FUMI SALAD

Salad

8 tablespoons slivered almonds, toasted
8 tablespoons sesame seeds, toasted
1 large head cabbage, chopped
8 green onions, chopped
2 packages ramen noodles

Dressing

4 tablespoons sugar
1 cup salad oil
6 tablespoons rice vinegar
1 teaspoon pepper
2 teaspoons salt

Toast almonds and sesame seeds in a dry skillet. Mix cabbage and onion in large bowl. Chill. Before serving, add sesame seeds, almonds, and noodles. Mix well. Mix dressing ingredients well. Pour dressing over salad and toss.

Variation: Add ginger to taste.

Yield: 24 servings.

BROCCOLI COLE SLAW

Slaw

1 package broccoli cole slaw
½ cup toasted almonds
½ cup sunflower seed kernels
3-4 chopped green onions
1 can rice noodles

Dressing

½ cup oil
¼ cup sugar
5 tablespoons apple cider vinegar
Salt and pepper

Mix dressing ahead. Just before serving, toss dressing with slaw mixture.

Yield: 6 to 8 servings.

CONFETTI COLE SLAW

1 small green cabbage, shredded
1 small onion, chopped
1 carrot, shredded
½ cup chopped green bell pepper
½ cup chopped red bell pepper
3 tablespoons chopped fresh parsley
½ cup cider vinegar
½ cup vegetable oil
3 tablespoons sugar
½ teaspoon salt
½ teaspoon white pepper

Combine first six ingredients in a bowl; set aside. Combine vinegar and next four ingredients; stir well. Add to cabbage mixture; toss gently. Cover and chill.

Yield: 6 to 8 servings.

POTATO SALAD DIANE

SALAD

- **5 pounds red potatoes, cooked and cut into ¼-inch pieces**
- **8 hard-cooked eggs, chopped**
- **2 cups celery, chopped**
- **1 cup carrots, chopped**
- **½ cup parsley, chopped**
- **1 cup green onions, chopped**
- **1 cup red bell pepper, chopped**

DRESSING

- **1 cup nonfat yogurt**
- **½ cup low-fat mayonnaise**
- **1 teaspoon Dijon mustard**
- **Dash of hot pepper sauce**
- **2 teaspoons Worcestershire sauce**
- **2 teaspoons celery seeds**
- **½ teaspoon garlic powder**
- **⅛ teaspoon white pepper**
- **1 teaspoon paprika**

Cook potatoes and cool. Leave skins on. Cut into ¼-inch pieces. Combine all vegetables. Combine all dressing ingredients except paprika. Toss together and sprinkle paprika on top. Refrigerate until ready to serve.

Yield: 8 servings.

DILLED POTATO SALAD

SALAD

3-4 pounds russet potatoes, peeled and cut into large pieces
2 bunches green onions, finely chopped
2 bunches fresh dill, finely chopped
Cherry tomato halves (garnish)

DRESSING

1 cup mayonnaise
⅓ cup sour cream
1 tablespoon red wine vinegar
1 tablespoon lemon pepper
1 tablespoon honey
1 tablespoon sugar
2-3 tablespoons sweet pickle juice, optional
½ teaspoon salt
Pepper to taste

Bring potatoes to boil and simmer just until cooked but still firm. Don't over cook. Drain in a colander and run cold water over potatoes. Drain again and set aside while preparing dressing. Whisk dressing ingredients until light and creamy. In a large mixing bowl, add potatoes, green onion and dill. Fold in the dressing. Mix well. Chill. Garnish with cherry tomatoes.

Yield: 8 to 10 servings.

ROASTED POTATO SALAD

4 cups quartered unpeeled small red potatoes
1 cup mayonnaise-type salad dressing
4 slices bacon, cooked crisp
2 hard-cooked eggs, chopped
¼ cup sliced green onions
¼ teaspoon salt
¼ teaspoon pepper
Nonstick spray

Heat oven to 425°. Place potatoes on a baking sheet sprayed with nonstick cooking spray. Bake for 30 to 35 minutes, or until potatoes are tender and golden brown, stirring once. Mix dressing, bacon, eggs, onions, salt and pepper in a large bowl. Add potatoes. Mix lightly. Serve warm or chilled.

Yield: 6 servings.

VIRGINIA'S TOMATO ASPIC

1 (6 ounce) package lemon flavored gelatin
2 cups tomato-vegetable juice cocktail
1 (10 ounce) can tomatoes with chiles, puréed
4 tablespoons white vinegar
1 (15 ounce) can drained English peas
1 cup diced celery
1 onion, finely chopped

Dissolve gelatin in simmering mixture of tomato-vegetable juice cocktail, tomatoes, and vinegar. Cool and add remaining ingredients. Pour into an 8 X 11½ X 2 inch dish and refrigerate until firm.

Hint: May serve with dressing consisting of 1 cup sour cream, 1 cup mayonnaise, and horseradish to taste.

Yield: 8 to 10 servings.

FANCY MUSTARD

1 (4 ounce) can dry mustard
1 cup white vinegar
2 eggs, beaten
1 cup sugar
Dash of salt

Mix mustard and vinegar and let it stand for 1 day. The next day, combine the remaining ingredients and add it to the mustard mixture. In a double boiler, bring water to a boil and cook mixture until it reaches custard consistency, stirring constantly. Cool and pour into sterilized jars.

Yield: 3 (8 ounce) jars.

PEPPER JELLY

3 large bell peppers
1½ cups cider vinegar
6½ cups sugar
2 tablespoons dried red pepper
1 bottle liquid fruit pectin
Green food color

Remove seeds from peppers, grind finely, and save juice and pulp (may be done in a blender). This will yield more than 1 cup. In a large pot, mix with vinegar, sugar, and red pepper. Bring to a rolling boil. Add liquid fruit pectin, bring to full rolling boil again, stirring constantly for 1 minute. Pour through fine mesh strainer into large mixing bowl and skim off foam. Add 3 drops green food coloring. If hotter jelly is desired, add cayenne pepper. Pour into hot, sterilized jars and seal.

Yield: 6 (8 ounce) jars.

BRANDIED CRANBERRY SAUCE

1 (12 ounce) bag of fresh cranberries
1½ cups sugar, divided
4 tablespoons brandy

Place cranberries on a cookie sheet. Sprinkle 1 cup of sugar over them. Cover tightly with foil. Bake 1 hour at 300°. Add the brandy and the rest of the sugar. Mix well. Place in container and refrigerate.

Hint: Serve with turkey, chicken or game.

Yield: 6 servings.

FROSTED RASPBERRY SALAD

1 (6 ounce) package raspberry gelatin
1 cup boiling water
1 (6 ounce) can cranberry sauce
1 (15¼ ounce) can crushed pineapple, drained
¾ cup port wine
1 (8 ounce) package cream cheese, softened
¼ cup sugar
1 (8 ounce) container sour cream
1 cup pecans, divided

Dissolve gelatin in boiling water. Stir in cranberry sauce until smooth. Stir in crushed, drained pineapple and port wine. Spoon mixture into a lightly oiled 12 X 8 X 2 inch pan. Chill until firm. Combine cream cheese, sugar, and sour cream. Reserve 2 tablespoons pecans and stir remaining cup into cream cheese mixture. Spread over gelatin. Sprinkle with remaining pecans and chill.

Yield: 8 to 10 servings.

FRESH CRANBERRY RELISH

¾ cup apple cider or juice
½-⅔ cup sugar
¼ teaspoon ground cinnamon
¼ teaspoon ground nutmeg
Dash of ground cloves
1 (12 ounce) package or 3 cups fresh cranberries
½ cup light raisins
½ cup chopped pecans

In a medium saucepan, combine juice, sugar, cinnamon, nutmeg and cloves. Cook and stir over medium heat until sugar is dissolved. Add cranberries and raisins. Bring to a boil and reduce heat. Stir in pecans. Transfer to a serving bowl. Cover and chill thoroughly until serving time.

Yield: 8 servings.

CRANBERRY SALAD

1 (15 ounce) can whole cranberry sauce
1 (3 ounce) package fruit flavored gelatin (orange, lemon, or cherry)
1 cup boiling water
¼ teaspoon salt
1 tablespoon lemon juice
½ cup mayonnaise
1 apple or orange, peeled and diced
¼ cup chopped walnuts

Heat cranberries, strain and set berries aside. Dissolve gelatin in hot juice and water. Add salt and lemon juice. Chill until it will mound. Beat mayonnaise with rotary beater until light and fluffy. Fold in fruit, cranberries, and nuts. Chill 4 hours or longer in a mold.

Hint: To freeze fresh cranberries, place unwashed in a freezer bag. Will keep up to 1 year.

Yield: 8 servings.

CRANBERRY CHUTNEY

4 cups fresh cranberries
2 cups sugar
1 cup water
½ teaspoon salt
6 whole cloves
2 sticks cinnamon
1 small onion, finely chopped
½ cup celery, finely chopped
1 cup raisins
1 apple, unpeeled, thinly sliced
1 pear, peeled, thinly sliced
1 lemon, seeded, finely chopped (including skin)
½ cup walnuts or almonds (do not use pecans)
⅓ cup candied ginger, chopped
Brandy or Cognac, to taste

Combine cranberries, sugar, water, salt, cloves, cinnamon, onions and celery in a large saucepan. Cook until berries begin to pop. Add raisins, apple, pear and lemon. Simmer slowly until mixture is thickened. Remove from heat and add nuts, candied ginger and brandy to taste.

Hint: Pack in small sterilized jars for gifts. The garnet red color is very enticing during the holidays.

Yield: 8 small jars.

COCKTAIL SAUCE

¼ cup chili sauce
½ cup ketchup
1-2 ounces lemon juice
½ teaspoon prepared horseradish

Mix ingredients together. Serve with boiled shrimp or crab.

Yield: 1 cup.

BASIL PESTO

2 cups fresh basil leaves
4 garlic cloves, peeled
¼ cup grated Parmesan cheese
1 cup extra virgin olive oil
1 cup chopped walnuts or pine nuts, optional

Put first three ingredients (and nuts if desired) in a blender or food processor. Add the olive oil and purée. Serve on pasta, tomatoes, etc. For soup and some sauces, omit the nuts.

Hint: Freezes well. Pour puréed mixture into ice cube trays and transfer to freezer bags when frozen. Then just drop a few into soups or sauces.

Yield: 8 servings.

FRENCH DRESSING

1 (10¾ ounce) can tomato soup
⅔ cup wine vinegar
3 teaspoons Worcestershire sauce
1 teaspoon salt
½ teaspoon pepper, coarse grind
1 clove garlic
1 cup salad oil
⅔ cup sugar
2 teaspoons mustard
2 tablespoons chopped onion

Blend all ingredients together well and shake before using. Keep refrigerated.

Yield: 1 quart.

CREAMY BASIL DRESSING

- 2 cups chopped fresh basil leaves, firmly packed
- ¼ cup olive oil
- 1 cup mayonnaise
- ¼ cup parsley, washed and stems removed
- 3 tablespoons balsamic vinegar
- 2 large cloves garlic
- ⅛ teaspoon dried tarragon
- ½ teaspoon dried mustard
- 3 green onions with tops, chopped

Combine all ingredients in a blender or food processor and season with salt and pepper.

Yield: 2 cups.

BALSAMIC DRESSING

- ½ cup balsamic vinegar
- 2 tablespoons olive oil
- 2 tablespoons Dijon-style mustard
- 1 tablespoon chopped fresh basil
- 1 teaspoon salt
- ¼ teaspoon ground pepper

Mix all ingredients well, preferably in a shaker.

Yield: ½ cup.

MANGO CHUTNEY

4-6 large mangoes
⅔ cup chopped onion
8 ounces raisins
1 cup chopped crystallized ginger (or 2 ounces peeled, finely chopped fresh ginger)
3 cups brown sugar
3 cups cider vinegar
2 tablespoons mustard seed
2 tablespoons chili powder
1 tablespoon salt

Dice mangoes. Place all ingredients in a medium sauce pan and cook over low heat, stirring occasionally, until reduced by one half and thickened to chutney consistency. Serve warm or room temperature.

Hint: Serve with pork or chicken.

Yield: 2 quarts.

JEZEBEL SAUCE

1 (2 ounce) can dry mustard
1 (8 ounce) jar pineapple preserves
1 (8 ounce) jar apple jelly
1 (6 ounce) jar horseradish

Combine all ingredients and mix well.

Hint: Serve as condiment for ham, roast, etc., glaze for chicken, or over cream cheese as a quick appetizer.

Yield: 2 cups.

MEAT MARINADE I

4 large garlic cloves, minced
4 tablespoons balsamic vinegar
4 tablespoons fresh lemon juice
3 tablespoons Dijon mustard
1½ tablespoons Worcestershire sauce
3 teaspoons herbes de Provence
½ teaspoon dried hot red pepper flakes
½ cup olive oil

Mix ingredients in a bowl. Place in a zip-top plastic bag. Add meat and marinate overnight in refrigerator.

Hint: Use for flank steak, London broil, or other meats.

Yield: Enough for 5 pounds meat.

MEAT MARINADE II

¼ cup vegetable oil
¼ cup balsamic vinegar
2 tablespoons barbecue sauce
1 tablespoon Worcestershire sauce
2 tablespoons whole black peppercorns
2 gloves of garlic
1 tablespoon fresh lemon juice

Place marinade in zip-top plastic bag. Add meat and marinate overnight in refrigerator.

Yield: Makes enough for 5 pounds meat.

MAYONNAISE FROM RIENZI

¼ teaspoon salt
¼ teaspoon dry mustard
¼ teaspoon red pepper
1 tablespoon tarragon vinegar
1 tablespoon lemon juice
1 cup olive oil, divided
1 egg

Combine all dry ingredients, vinegar, and lemon juice in a blender. Blend. Turn off blender and pour ⅓ cup of olive oil into mixture. Then add egg. Start blender again. With machine running, pour remaining ⅔ cups oil slowly into mixture.

Yield: 1 cup.

MARIANNA'S MUSTARD SAUCE

½ cup brown sugar
⅓ cup prepared mustard
2 eggs
2 tablespoons butter, softened
⅓ cup cider vinegar

In a small, heavy saucepan whisk sugar, mustard, eggs, and butter with whisk. Gradually whisk in vinegar. Cook over low heat stirring constantly until slightly thickened, 8 to 10 minutes. Cool to room temperature or refrigerate until cold.

Hint: Serve with baked ham or pork.

Yield: 1½ cups.

PASTA & CASSEROLE COLLECTION

Pietro Paolo Bonzi, Italian, 1576-1640
The Fruit Market, c. 1625-30
Oil on canvas, 47½ x 71 in.
The Sarah Campbell Blaffer Foundation, Houston, Texas

In a brilliant and formal composition, Bonzi creates an elaborate and seemingly random display of fruits and vegetables, using contrasts abundantly. The striking use of light detailing the smooth skins on the apples and rough surfaces on the pumpkins and peaches and the sharp contrast of purple fruit on a white cloth are reminiscent of Carravaggio. The pomegranates are bursting with succulence even as the lifeless body of the rooster totters precariously in the basket. The viewer sees the fruit display from an elevated vantage point while the market personnel, in typical Tuscan-style clothing, are seen from a lowered perspective. The still life elements dominate the composition both spatially and with the use of color counterpoints.

Pasta & Casserole Collection

Portofino Primavera
Fettuccine Primavera
Pasta with Sun-Dried Tomato
Spinach Pasta Shells
Spaghetti with Roasted Eggplant and Tomatoes
Stuffed Ziti
Macaroni and Cheese
Sausage and Mostaccioli Bake
4-Star Pasta
Olive Fettuccine
Debbie's Noodle Kugel
Greek-Style Chicken and Penne Salad
Spicy Fettuccine with Crawfish

PORTOFINO PRIMAVERA

2 tablespoons olive oil
1 cup chopped onion
1 large garlic clove, minced
1¾ cups tomatoes (14½ ounce can)
⅔ cup tomato paste (6 ounce can)
1 cup chicken broth or water
1 cup zucchini, sliced and quartered
½ cup sliced ripe olives, drained
2 tablespoons capers
½ teaspoon salt, or to taste
1 pound dry pasta, cooked according to package directions

In a medium saucepan, heat oil. Sauté onion and garlic for 1 minute. Add tomatoes and juice, tomato paste, chicken broth or water, zucchini, olives, capers and salt. Bring to a boil. Reduce heat and simmer, uncovered, for 15 to 20 minutes. Serve over pasta.

Yield: 4 cups.

FETTUCCINE PRIMAVERA

2 cups small broccoli flowerets
1 cup carrots, thinly sliced
½ cup green onions, sliced
2 cloves garlic, minced
3 tablespoons fresh basil, chopped
¼ cup olive oil
2 cups fresh mushrooms, sliced
¼ teaspoon salt
¼ teaspoon pepper
½ cup dry white wine
3½ cups cooked fettuccine

Sauté first 5 ingredients in olive oil in a large skillet for 5 minutes or until vegetables are crisp and tender, stirring often. Add mushrooms, salt, pepper and wine; cook 2 minutes or until mushrooms are tender. Gently toss with fettuccine.

Yield: 2 servings.

PASTA WITH SUN-DRIED TOMATOES

1 pound fresh angel hair pasta or fettuccini
4 ounces feta cheese
2-3 large garlic cloves, pressed
1 (8 ounce) jar sun-dried tomatoes in olive oil, chopped
Toasted pine nuts, optional
¼ pound blanched broccoli flowerets, optional

Cook and drain pasta. Crumble feta cheese over pasta. Add garlic to pasta. Drain tomatoes, reserve oil, chop tomatoes. Add sun-dried tomatoes along with oil, as desired, and toss together. Toast pine nuts in oven or skillet until golden. Add pine nuts and broccoli, if desired. Serve at room temperature.

Yield: 8 servings.

SPINACH PASTA SHELLS

12 jumbo pasta shells (about 6 ounces), uncooked
1 (10 ounce) package frozen chopped spinach, thawed (reserve liquid)
½ cup toasted wheat germ (can substitute breadcrumbs)
½ cup finely shredded Parmesan cheese
1 green onion, thinly sliced
½ cup finely chopped walnuts, toasted
¼ teaspoon ground nutmeg
⅓ cup water
1 (28 ounce) jar Alfredo or spaghetti sauce

Heat oven to 350°. Lightly spray 8 inch baking dish with cooking spray. Cook shells according to package directions; drain and cool. In large bowl, combine spinach, reserved liquid, wheat germ, cheese, onions, walnuts, nutmeg and water. Spread ½ cup sauce in bottom of baking dish. Spoon spinach mixture into cooled shells, dividing equally. Arrange in baking dish; pour remaining sauce over shells. Cover and bake 30 to 35 minutes or until sauce is bubbly and shells are heated through. Remove from oven and serve.

Yield: 6 servings.

SPAGHETTI WITH ROASTED EGGPLANT AND TOMATOES

1-1¼ pounds eggplant, trimmed and halved lengthwise
⅓ cup olive oil
1 onion, minced
2 large cloves garlic, minced
1 (28 ounce) can crushed tomatoes in puree
Salt and pepper
1 pound spaghetti
2 tablespoons fresh mint basil

Preheat oven to 400°. Arrange the eggplant, cut-side down on an oiled baking sheet and bake until tender, about 20 to 25 minutes. Let cool, remove the skin, and coarsely chop the pulp. In a skillet over medium Add the tomatoes and simmer, stirring occasionally, for 10 to 12 minutes or until thick. Add the chopped eggplant and salt and pepper and simmer, stirring occasionally, for 5 minutes or until heated through. Stir in the basil. Keep the sauce warm. Bring a large saucepan of salted water to a boil. Add the spaghetti and cook until al dente. Drain, transfer to a heated bowl, and toss gently with the sauce.

Yield: 4 to 6 servings.

STUFFED ZITI

1 (10-12 ounce) package of ziti noodles
1 package frozen spinach soufflé, thawed
1 (15 ounce) jar spaghetti sauce
1 cup cottage or ricotta cheese
1 (4 ounce) package shredded mozzarella cheese
2 ounces grated Parmesan cheese

Boil pasta about 6 to 8 minutes. Drain. Combine spinach soufflé, spaghetti sauce and cottage or ricotta cheese and beat thoroughly. Blend in drained pasta. Pour into casserole. Bake at 350° for 20 to 30 minutes. Top with mozzarella cheese and sprinkle with Parmesan. Place under broiler until cheese melts and browns, 2 to 3 minutes.

Yield: 2 to 4 servings.

MACARONI AND CHEESE

1 (12 ounce) package elbow macaroni
1 (12 ounce) package shredded sharp cheddar cheese
1 (8 ounce) package shredded mild cheddar cheese
1 pint half-and-half
1 tablespoon flour
Butter to taste
Salt and pepper to taste

Cook elbow macaroni according to package directions. Drain. Toss with butter, salt and pepper. In a blender, put sharp cheese, half-and-half that has been warmed (2 minutes in microwave with the top opened), flour and more salt to taste. Blend. Pour over macaroni, stir to mix well. Pour into a glass baking dish and top with the shredded mild cheese. Bake at 350° until bubbly and cheese on top is melted (approximately 20 minutes).

Yield: 4 servings.

SAUSAGE AND MOSTACCIOLI BAKE

½ pound package of mostaccioli, uncooked
1 pound fully cooked smoked sausage (sliced ¼ inch thick)
1 (10¾ ounce) can cream of chicken soup, undiluted
½ cup sour cream
¼ cup milk
1 teaspoon parsley flakes
½ teaspoon salt
8-10 drops hot pepper sauce
½ cup diced Monterey Jack cheese
½ cup diced cheddar cheese

Prepare mostaccioli according to package directions; drain. In medium skillet, brown sausage; drain. In medium bowl, blend soup, sour cream, milk, parsley flakes, salt and hot pepper sauce. Add mostaccioli and cheese; mix well. Pour into greased 9 X 9 inch baking dish. Top with smoked sausage. Bake at 350° until hot, about 30 minutes.

Yield: 4 to 6 servings.

4 STAR PASTA

½ cup olive oil
8 cloves garlic
2 pounds ripe plum tomatoes, chopped
2 medium zucchini, matchstick pieces
2 medium red peppers, thin strips (can use 1 yellow and 1 red)
1 pound Fusilli or rotelle pasta
8 large green onions, thinly sliced (include 2 inches of green)
1½ cups fresh basil, chopped
1 teaspoon salt
1 teaspoon pepper
2 cups grated Parmesan cheese

Preheat oven to 375°. In a large baking dish, combine olive oil and garlic cloves and bake for 10 to 15 minutes until garlic is golden. Remove from oven and discard garlic. Add tomatoes, zucchini, and peppers to baking dish; toss and return to oven for 10 minutes. Meanwhile, cook pasta al dente; drain. Add pasta to baking dish with green onions, basil, salt and pepper and approximately ½ to ¾ cup of grated cheese. Toss well and serve at room temperature. Sprinkle with remaining cheese.

Note: This is great served with grilled sausage.

Yield: 8 servings.

OLIVE FETTUCCINE

12 ounces fettuccine, cooked
¼ cup olive oil
2 cloves garlic, minced
3 ounces green olives, sliced
6 ounces black olives, sliced
Small bunch parsley, chopped
½ teaspoon crushed red pepper
½ cup water
¼ cup Parmesan cheese

Cook fettuccine. Sauté garlic in olive oil. Add remaining ingredients, except cheese. Simmer 10 minutes. Stir into pasta. Top with cheese.

Yield: 4 to 6 servings.

DEBBIE'S NOODLE KUGEL

1 (16 ounce) package wide noodles
¾ cup butter, softened
12 ounces cream cheese, softened
1 cup sugar
2 teaspoons vanilla
1 teaspoon cinnamon
1 pint sour cream
6 eggs
1 cup frosted corn flakes, crushed

Preheat oven to 350° Cook noodles al dente and drain. Cream butter, cream cheese, sugar, vanilla, and cinnamon until smooth. Add sour cream and eggs. Beat until well mixed. Add in noodles and mix well. Pour into greased 13 X 9 X 2 inch glass casserole dish. Sprinkle with crushed frosted corn flakes. Can drizzle melted butter on top. Bake until firm and golden on top, approximately 50 minutes.

Yield: 10 to 12 servings.

GREEK-STYLE CHICKEN AND PENNE SALAD

Salad

6 ounces (2 cups) uncooked dried penne pasta
1 tablespoon butter
½ cup chopped red onion
1 teaspoon finely chopped fresh garlic
1 pound chicken stir-fry meat
1 (14 ounce) can artichoke hearts, drained, coarsely chopped
1 medium tomato, chopped
3 ounces (½ cup) tomato and basil-seasoned feta cheese, crumbled
2 tablespoons chopped fresh parsley
2 tablespoons fresh lemon juice
1 teaspoon dried oregano leaves
½ bunch chopped dill

Dressing

2 tablespoons mayonnaise
3 tablespoons white wine vinegar
2 tablespoons Dijon mustard
⅔ cup olive oil

Cook pasta according to package directions. Drain. Meanwhile, in a 10 inch nonstick skillet, melt butter until sizzling; add onion and garlic. Cook over medium-high heat 2 minutes. Add chicken. Continue cooking, stirring occasionally, until golden brown (5 to 6 minutes). Reduce heat to medium-low. Add cooked pasta and all remaining ingredients; toss gently. Cook until heated through (2 to 3 minutes). Mix first 3 ingredients of dressing together. Whisk in olive oil gradually until well blended. Mix dressing into cooled pasta mixture. Season with salt and pepper if desired.

Yield: 8 to 10 servings.

SPICY FETTUCCINE WITH CRAWFISH

4 ounces fettuccine
8 tablespoons butter
⅓ cup green bell pepper, diced
⅓ cup red bell pepper, diced
½ cup onion, chopped
8 ounces cooked crawfish tails, peeled or ½ pound small shrimp, peeled
¾ teaspoon Creole or Cajun seasoning
¼ teaspoon dried crushed red pepper
⅓ cup diced canned tomatoes
2 tablespoons sliced green onions

Cook fettuccine until tender but firm. Meanwhile, melt 2 tablespoons butter in large skillet over high heat. Add bell peppers and onions, sauté until almost soft, about 3 minutes. Add crawfish, Creole seasoning and red pepper. Sauté until crawfish are heated through, about 1 to 2 minutes. Add tomatoes and onions and cook until heated through. Remove skillet from heat and gradually add remaining 6 tablespoons butter, whisking until melted. Season with salt and pepper.

Yield: 2 servings

VEGETABLE COLLECTION

James Peale, American, 1749-1831
Still Life with Vegetables, 1826
Oil on canvas, 20 x 26½ in.
The Museum of Fine Arts, Houston, the Bayou Bend Collection, museum purchase with funds provided by the Theta Charity Antiques Show in honor of Mrs. Fred T. Couper, Jr.

James Peale was known primarily as a miniaturist but is also regarded as the founder of the still-life tradition in America along with his brother, preeminent American painter Charles Willson Peale, and nephew Raphaelle Peale. Though considered a "lowly" subject for art, this still life takes the ordinary and elevates it through careful and sensitive balance of color and light. The warm and rich colors of the turnips, tomatoes, radishes and squash seem to glow in this golden light even as it highlights the graceful and fluid movement of the leaves and tendrils.

Vegetable Collection

Grilled Asparagus

Sweet 'n' Sour Asparagus

Three Corn Casserole

Vidalia Onion Pie

Eggplant, Red Pepper and Feta Gratin

Potatoes Baked with Tomatoes

Carrots in Mustard Dill Sauce

Sweet Potato Soufflé

Hash Brown Potato Casserole

Leona's Potato Pancakes

Patio Potatoes

Fix Ahead Mashed Potatoes

Armenian Pilaf

Wild Rice, Cranberry Pilaf

Cumin Rice

Spinach and Rice Casserole

Spinach Casserole

Calabacitas

Summer Squash Sauté

Stuffed Acorn Squash

Baked Cushaw

Yellow Squash and Cornbread Casserole

Yellow Squash Patties

Mushroom Stuffing

Italian Zucchini and Tomatoes with Garlic

Southwestern Dressing

Turnip Soufflé

GRILLED ASPARAGUS

1 pound asparagus
½ cup olive oil
½ cup balsamic vinegar
2 chopped green onions
1 tablespoon prepared Dijon mustard
1 tablespoon lemon juice
1 tablespoon chopped fresh thyme
1 teaspoon rosemary
Salt and pepper to taste

Rinse asparagus and place in large plastic bag. Add remaining ingredients for marinade. Marinate in refrigerator for several hours. Remove asparagus from marinade. Reserve marinade. Arrange asparagus in a grilling basket. Grill over hot coals, turning and basting with reserved marinade, until slightly charred.

Yield: 4 servings.

SWEET 'N' SOUR ASPARAGUS

3 pounds fresh asparagus
⅔ cup white vinegar
½ cup sugar
½ teaspoon salt
1 teaspoon cloves
3 sticks cinnamon
1 tablespoon celery seed
½ cup water
1 hard-cooked egg, grated

Slightly steam asparagus, maintaining firmness, then place asparagus into a baking dish. Mix vinegar, sugar, salt, and spices in a saucepan with the water and bring to a boil. Pour boiling hot liquid over the asparagus. Cover and refrigerate 24 hours. To serve, pour off liquid and sprinkle with grated eggs.

Yield: 4 to 6 servings.

THREE CORN CASSEROLE

1 stick (1/4 pound) margarine
1 (12 ounce) can whole kernel corn, drained
1 (17 ounce) can cream style corn
1 (8 ounce) package corn muffin mix
1 cup sour cream
1 egg

Heat oven to 350°. Melt margarine in 2½ or 3 quart dish. Set aside to cool. Mix together 2 cans corn, muffin mix, sour cream and egg. Add margarine and mix well. Pour into a greased baking dish. Bake at 350° for 35 to 40 minutes or until set.

Yield: 10 to 12 servings.

VIDALIA ONION PIE

1½ cups finely crushed buttery crackers
6 tablespoons unsalted butter, room temperature
2 cups thinly sliced Vidalia onions or 1015 onions
¾ cup whole milk
2 eggs
¾ teaspoon salt
Pepper to taste
¾ cup grated sharp cheddar cheese
Paprika

Preheat oven to 350°. Mix crackers and 4 tablespoons butter in a bowl until well blended. Press onto bottom and up 1-inch on the sides of an 8-inch pie plate. Melt remaining 2 tablespoons butter in heavy skillet over medium heat. Add onions and sauté until tender, about 12 minutes. Arrange onions on cracker crust. Beat milk, eggs, and salt. Season with pepper. Pour over onions. Sprinkle cheese over filling. Sprinkle with paprika. Bake pie until knife comes out clean, about 35 minutes.

Yield: 8 servings.

EGGPLANT, RED PEPPER AND FETA GRATIN

3 red bell peppers
2 pounds eggplant, cut diagonally in ½-inch slices
5 tablespoons olive oil
2 medium onions, thinly sliced
2 garlic cloves, minced
½ cup loosely packed fresh basil
½ cup crumbled feta cheese
Salt and pepper to taste

Broil peppers under preheated broiler about 2 inches from heat, turning every 5 minutes, until skins are blistered and charred. Remove from oven and cover until cool enough to handle. Keeping peppers whole, peel them, starting at the blossom end. Quarter lengthwise, reserving juices in a bowl, and cut into 3 X 2-inch slices.

Halve eggplant slices crosswise if very large. In a kettle of boiling water cook eggplant in batches, pressing down with back of large spoon to keep submerged, until tender, 5 to 10 minutes, and drain in colander 10 minutes. Preheat oven to 400°.

In a non-stick skillet, heat 2 tablespoons oil over moderate heat until hot but not smoking and cook onions and garlic, stirring occasionally, 10 minutes. Spread onion mixture on bottom of a 3 quart gratin or other shallow baking pan. Arrange a row of tightly overlapping eggplant slices over onion mixture across one end of baking dish and slip a basil leaf between each slice. Arrange a row of tightly overlapping pepper slices next to eggplant and continue making alternating rows of eggplants and peppers in same manner. Season vegetables with salt and pepper and drizzle reserved pepper juices and remaining 3 tablespoons oil. Bake gratin in middle of oven 45 minutes, pressing down on vegetables occasionally with back of large spoon and basting with cooking liquid. Sprinkle with feta cheese and continue baking until cheese is melted and golden, about 10 minutes more.

Yield: 8 servings.

POTATOES BAKED WITH TOMATOES

2 large, red or yellow onions, thinly sliced
2 pounds potatoes, peeled and thinly sliced
1 pound tomatoes sliced, with their juice (or 1 large can)
6 tablespoons olive oil
1 cup freshly grated Parmesan or Romano cheese
Salt and freshly ground black pepper, to taste
A few leaves of fresh basil, torn into pieces
¼ cup water

Preheat oven to 350°. Brush a large baking dish generously with oil. Arrange a layer of onions in the dish, followed by layers of potatoes and tomatoes. Pour on a little oil and sprinkle with the cheese. Season with salt and pepper. Tear basil leaves and add a few to this layer. Repeat until the vegetables are used up, ending with an overlapping layer of potatoes and tomatoes. Add torn basil leaves here and there among the vegetables. Sprinkle the top with cheese and a little oil. Pour water over dish. Bake for 1 to 1½ hours, or until tender. If the top begins to brown too much, place a sheet of foil or a flat cookie sheet on top of the dish. Serve hot.

Yield: 6 servings.

CARROTS IN MUSTARD DILL SAUCE

½ pound carrots, cut in 2 X ½ inch julienne strips
¼ cup mayonnaise
¼ cup plain yogurt
1 teaspoon Dijon mustard
2 tablespoons fresh chopped dillweed
Salt and pepper to taste

Steam carrots in a covered vegetable steamer for 6 minutes or until just tender. In a small bowl whisk together mayonnaise, yogurt, mustard, dill and salt and pepper. Stir in carrots and let the mixture stand until the carrots are at room temperature.

Yield: 4 servings.

SWEET POTATO SOUFFLÉ

2 cups mashed sweet potato (drain first if using canned)
2 eggs, beaten
1¼ cups sugar
1¼ sticks butter or margarine, melted and divided
1 cup milk
½ teaspoon nutmeg
½ teaspoon cinnamon
¾ cup crushed corn flakes
½ cup brown sugar
½ cup chopped nuts

Mix potatoes, eggs, sugar, half of butter, milk, nutmeg, and cinnamon. Pour into a greased casserole. Bake at 400° for 20 to 25 minutes. Mix corn flakes, brown sugar, nuts and remaining butter. Spread over casserole and bake for 10 minutes.

Yield: 10 to 12 servings.

HASH BROWN POTATO CASSEROLE

2 (10¾ ounce) cans condensed cream of potato soup, undiluted
1 cup sour cream
½ teaspoon garlic salt
1 (1 pound) package frozen hash brown potatoes
2 cups shredded cheddar cheese
½ cup grated Parmesan cheese

In a large bowl, combine the soup, sour cream and garlic salt. Add potatoes and cheddar cheese; mix well. Pour into a greased 13 X 9 inch baking dish. Top with Parmesan cheese. Bake, uncovered, at 350° for 55-60 minutes or until potatoes are tender.

Variation: Can top with 1 cup Italian breadcrumbs before baking.

Yield: 12 to 14 servings.

LEONA'S POTATO PANCAKES

6 slices white bread
1 very large yellow onion
3 cups potatoes, cubed
2 eggs
1 teaspoon salt
½ teaspoon pepper
Cooking oil
Applesauce
Sour cream

In food processor, process bread to make fresh breadcrumbs. Grate onion and potatoes together in food processor. Drain any liquid. Mix with eggs and then add breadcrumbs, salt and pepper. Fry in a small amount of hot oil. Serve with applesauce and sour cream.

Yield: approximately 25 pancakes.

PATIO POTATOES

4 medium baking potatoes
1 cup cottage cheese
1 cup sour cream
¼ cup chopped green onions
1 tablespoons butter
Salt and pepper to taste
¼ cup grated Parmesan cheese
Butter

Cook potatoes in skins. Cool, peel, and mash. Add cottage cheese, sour cream, green onions, butter, and salt and pepper to taste. Whip. Turn into buttered casserole. Dot with butter and sprinkle with Parmesan. Bake at 350° for 25 minutes until gold brown.

Yield: 6 to 8 servings.

FIX AHEAD MASHED POTATOES

3 pounds potatoes
2 tablespoons butter
2 (3 ounce) packages cream cheese
⅔ cup sour cream
¼ cup milk
½ teaspoon salt
1 tablespoon melted butter
Salt and pepper

Boil potatoes in skins in salted water, to cover, for 25 minutes. Peel and mash. Whip. Add 2 tablespoons butter and next 3 ingredients. Mix until blended. Salt and pepper to taste. Spoon into baking dish. Brush with melted butter. Bake immediately or refrigerate. If refrigerated, let stand at room temperature 30 minutes before baking. Bake at 350°, uncovered for 30 minutes.

Yield: 8 servings.

ARMENIAN PILAF

½ cup unsalted butter
½ cup vermicelli or fine noodles, crushed into ¼-inch pieces
1 cup uncooked long-grain rice
2 cups chicken broth
⅛ teaspoon garlic powder
1 teaspoon salt

Melt butter in skillet, add vermicelli and sauté over moderate heat until browned. Watch carefully so noodles do not burn. Rinse rice in cold water until water is clear, add to skillet and sauté. Add chicken broth, garlic powder, and salt. Cover tightly and cook on low heat for 25 minutes or until broth has been absorbed and rice is cooked.

Yield: 6 servings.

WILD RICE AND CRANBERRY PILAF

⅔ cup wild rice
3 cups water
Pinch of salt
2 tablespoons butter
¼ cup dried cranberries
¼ cup chopped toasted walnuts
2 tablespoons fresh parsley
Salt and pepper to taste

Rinse wild rice under cold water. Place in water with a pinch of salt. Bring to boil, stir and reduce heat and simmer slowly for 45 minutes. Remove from heat and add butter. Add cranberries, walnuts and parsley. Season with salt and pepper. Serve hot or cold.

Yield: 4 servings.

CUMIN RICE

2 tablespoons butter
¼ cup finely chopped onion
1 teaspoon minced garlic
1 cup uncooked rice
½ teaspoon ground cumin
Salt and freshly ground pepper to taste
1½ cups chicken broth
2 sprigs parsley
2 sprigs fresh thyme or ½ teaspoon dried
1 bay leaf

Melt 1 tablespoon butter in a heavy saucepan with a tight fitting lid. Add onions and garlic and cook, stirring until onions are wilted. Add the rice, cumin, salt and pepper. Stir briefly over low heat until the grains are coated with butter. Stir in the broth, making sure there are no lumps in the rice. Add parsley, thyme, and bay leaf. Bring to a boil. Cover and simmer over low heat for 17 minutes. Discard bay leaf, parsley and thyme. Using a fork, stir in remaining butter,

Yield: 4 servings.

SPINACH AND RICE CASSEROLE

3 cups cooked rice
1 (10 ounce) package frozen, chopped spinach, cooked as directed and drained
⅓ cup chopped fresh parsley
2 eggs, well beaten
½ cup grated cheddar cheese
1 teaspoon salt
1 cup milk
¼ cup butter, cut into pieces
1 teaspoon grated onion

Put rice, spinach, parsley, eggs and cheese into an ovenproof casserole dish. Stir in remaining ingredients. Bake at 350° for 45 minutes.

Yield: 6 to 8 servings.

SPINACH CASSEROLE

1 (8½ ounce) can artichoke hearts, drained
2 (10 ounce) packages of frozen, chopped spinach; cooked as directed and drained
1 (8 ounce) can sliced water chestnuts, drained
½ stick butter
2 tablespoons chopped onion, optional
2 (3 ounce) packages cream cheese
Breadcrumbs

Cut drained artichokes in half and place in the bottom of a greased 13 X 9 X 2 inch baking dish. Sauté onion in butter until onion is translucent. Add cream cheese and cook over medium heat until cheese is melted. Add spinach and water chestnuts and mix well. Pour spinach mixture over artichokes and sprinkle with breadcrumbs. Bake at 350° for 25 minutes.

Yield: 4 to 6 servings.

CALABACITAS

1 yellow onion, chopped
2-3 small zucchini, sliced into ¼-inch rounds
2-3 small yellow squash, sliced into ¼-inch rounds
1-2 ears corn, cooked and cut from cobs
½ cup green chiles
1 fresh tomato, diced (optional)
¼ cup olive oil
Grated cheese (cheddar, Monterey Jack, or mixture)

Sauté the onion and squashes in olive oil. Add the green chiles, corn and the tomatoes (if desired). Simmer the mixture until the vegetables are tender or bake for 15 to 20 minutes at 350°. Season to taste. Top with grated cheese.

Hint: This is a traditional New Mexico summer dish straight from the garden. The vegetables can be varied to suit the cook and the garden.

Yield: 6 to 8 servings.

SUMMER SQUASH SAUTÉ

1 sliced red onion
2 tablespoons olive oil
1 yellow squash, sliced lengthwise then cut into ¼-inch slices
1 green zucchini, sliced lengthwise then cut into ¼-inch slices
2 cups sliced mushrooms
1 teaspoon fresh rosemary, chopped
1 teaspoon minced garlic
Salt and pepper
2 tablespoons fresh lemon juice

In large skillet, sauté sliced red onion in olive oil over medium heat for 2 minutes. Add squash and zucchini to onion with sliced mushrooms. Season with rosemary and garlic and sauté for 5 more minutes stirring occasionally. Add salt and pepper, if desired. Transfer to serving platter and sprinkle with lemon juice.

Yield: 4 servings.

STUFFED ACORN SQUASH

2 medium acorn squash
1 small bunch green onions, chopped (6 to 8)
3 tablespoons butter
½ cup sour cream
1 (8 ounce) package cream cheese (not whipped)
Salt and white pepper to taste
Grated Parmesan cheese
4 slices bacon, fried crisp and crumbled (optional)

Wash and cut squash in half. Remove seeds. Place squash, cut side down, in glass dish with ¼ cup water and microwave for approximately 8 minutes or until pulp is tender. Remove and let cool slightly. Sauté onions in butter. Scoop out squash pulp and arrange squash shells in baking dish. Mash squash pulp and mix with onions. Add sour cream, cream cheese, and seasonings to taste. Mix thoroughly. Fill squash shells, top with dab of butter and Parmesan cheese. (Optional: Sprinkle fried crisp and crumbled bacon on top). Bake at 350° for 15 minutes.

Variation: For a main dish, add cooked ground beef with mashed squash and other ingredients before baking.

Yield: 4 servings.

BAKED CUSHAW

1 medium cushaw, or other crookneck squash
1 stick butter
6 eggs
1 cup brown sugar
1 cup white sugar
1 teaspoon salt
½ teaspoon cinnamon
¼ teaspoon nutmeg

Peel cushaw and cut into chunks. Place in large pot. Add water and cook covered until soft. Drain liquid and mash with potato masher. Add butter, beaten eggs, sugars, and salt. Add spices; mix well. Bake in greased casserole at 350° for 45 minutes.

Yield: 4 servings.

YELLOW SQUASH AND CORNBREAD CASSEROLE

3 pounds yellow squash (8-10)
1 (10¾ ounce) can condensed cream of chicken soup, undiluted
Salt and pepper
¼ cup chopped onion
½ cup sour cream
1 stick butter or margarine (melted)
⅔ of a (8 ounce) package corn bread stuffing mix

Preheat oven to 350°. Cut squash into quarters and steam with a little water until soft. Mash. In a large bowl, combine squash with soup, salt and pepper, chopped onion, and sour cream. Place mixture in a 1½ quart casserole. In a small bowl, combine melted butter and stuffing mix. Mix well and sprinkle over casserole. Cover and bake until bubbly and hot, about 30 minutes.

Yield: 10 to 12 servings.

YELLOW SQUASH PATTIES

¾ pound small yellow squash, thinly sliced (about 4)
1 egg, beaten
¼ cup all-purpose flour
½ teaspoon baking powder
¼ teaspoon salt
⅓ cup plus 2 tablespoons corn bread mix
1 medium onion, finely chopped
Vegetable oil

Cook squash in a small amount of boiling water 10 to 15 minutes or until tender. Drain well. Mash enough squash to measure about 1 heaping cup. Combine the 1 cup squash with beaten egg and mix well. Sift flour, baking powder, and salt together. Add corn bread mix and combine. Add squash mixture and onion to dry ingredients and stir until blended. Drop mixture by level tablespoons into hot oil. Cook until golden brown, turning once. Drain well on paper towels.

Yield: 2 dozen.

MUSHROOM STUFFING

1 pound fresh mushrooms, finely chopped
1-2 tablespoons onion, diced
4 tablespoons butter
Salt and pepper to taste
1 (8 ounce) package cream cheese
Nutmeg, optional

Sauté mushrooms and onion in butter, salt and pepper. After most of liquid cooks away, add cream cheese. Mix and spoon into casserole dish. Bake at 350° for 25 minutes. If desired, sprinkle with nutmeg before baking.

Hint: Can be used as stuffing for breast of veal or whole chicken.

Yield: 2 to 4 servings.

ITALIAN ZUCCHINI AND TOMATOES WITH GARLIC

2 zucchini sliced into ⅓-inch slices
2 medium tomatoes cut into 8 wedges each
1 tablespoon olive oil
4 or more pods garlic, thinly sliced
Salt and pepper to taste
Fresh oregano leaves to taste
Freshly grated Parmesan cheese, if desired

Heat olive oil in skillet. Add zucchini and sauté for a few minutes until halfway done. Add tomatoes, garlic, salt, pepper, and oregano and sauté until softened, about 1 to 2 minutes. Serve with Parmesan cheese, if desired.

Note: May use dried oregano or Italian herb mix.

Hint: Do not over cook. Zucchini should still be bright green and not mushy. Garlic and oregano will be sweeter if not overcooked.

Yield: 2 to 4 servings.

SOUTHWESTERN DRESSING

2-3 cups cubed white bread
1 recipe corn bread, broken into large pieces
¾ cup chopped onion
¾ cup chopped celery
⅓-½ cup chopped bell pepper
2 tablespoons chopped fresh parsley
1-2 teaspoons poultry seasoning
1 teaspoon dried leaf sage
4 eggs
6 cups chicken broth
Salt and pepper to taste
12 tamales, broken up
½ cup melted butter

In a large mixing bowl, combine white bread and cornbread. Sauté onion, celery, and bell pepper in a little oil. Add to mixing bowl, along with parsley, poultry seasoning, and sage. Lightly beat the eggs and fold them into mixture. Add salt and pepper and 2-3 cups chicken broth; add the tamales. Place in a greased 13 X 9 inch pan. Don't pack down. Pour remaining broth and melted butter over stuffing. There will be a lot of liquid. Bake at 350° for 1 hour. Cover loosely with foil and bake another 30 minutes, or until all liquid is absorbed.

Yield: 10 to 12 servings.

TURNIP SOUFFLÉ

10 small turnips
2 carrots
1 egg
1 tablespoon milk
1 teaspoon sugar
2 tablespoons butter
1 tablespoons bacon fat
Salt and pepper to taste
Breadcrumbs

Slice carrots and turnips, combine in a saucepan and boil in a small amount of salted water until tender. Drain and mash. Stir in egg, milk, sugar, butter, bacon fat, salt and pepper and place in greased, 1-quart casserole. Top with breadcrumbs. Bake 30 minutes at 350°.

Yield: 6 to 8 servings.

MEAT COLLECTION

Willem Claesz. Heda, Dutch, 1594-1680
Banquet Piece with Ham, 1656
Oil on canvas, 44 x 60 in.
The Museum of Fine Arts, Houston, gift of Mr. and Mrs. Raymond H. Goodrich

Heda was the leading representative of the Dutch school of still life painting. His arrangements of objects were monochromatic and most frequently arranged so to appear as though breakfast had been abruptly interrupted and abandoned. In these still lifes he juxtaposes the smooth surface of crystal and silver with the rough surface of oyster shells, and places it first on a linen tablecloth, then a velvet cloth and finally on a hard rough table. He then sets it against a blank and unknown background upon which light falls softly from an unknown source. The pink ham, the light blue of the Delft bowl and the pale yellowed bread, just subtly interrupts the monochrome theme. The peel of the lemon breaks the picture plane as it falls from the composition.

Meat Collection

Standing Rib Roast
Easy Chateau Stroganoff
Filet Mignon
Great Brisket
Teriyaki
Bob's New York Corned Beef
Flambéed Pepper Steak
Kathryn's Stew
Texas Stew
Oven Beef Stew
Chili
Peter Marzio's Famous Lasagna
Beef and Cheddar Loaf
Moist Meat Loaf
Eggplant Moussake
Béchamel Sauce
Macaroni Pastitsio with Phyllo Pastry (Pastilla)
Sweet and Sour Cabbage Rolls
Veal Cutlets Parmesan
Zurich Geschnetzeltes (Veal)
Grillades
Spicy Braised Pork
Twice-Cooked Pork with Cabbage and Sai Fun
Marinated Pork Tenderloin
Pork Tenderloin Medallions
Ron's Pork Chops
Pork Tenderloin with Apple and Red Chile Chutney
Gourmet Pork Filet
Lamb Shanks a la Merrily
Lamb and White Bean Ragoût

STANDING RIB ROAST

1 5-rib, fully trimmed, rib roast
2 tablespoons butter, softened
2 medium carrots, roughly chopped
2 medium onions, roughly chopped
2 cups excellent beef broth

Hint: You will need a reliable meat thermometer, a low-sided roasting pan, and a rack to fit the pan.

Leave the meat out at room temperature for an hour before it is to go into the oven. Preheat oven to 325°. Rub cut ends of beef with butter and place it fat side up (ribs down) on the rack in the roasting pan. Roast approximately 2½ hours. Baste the cut ends with accumulated fat from the roasting pan every half hour. An hour before end of roasting time, scatter the chopped vegetables into the pan. Half an hour later, start checking temperature. When the thermometer reaches 105°, watch closely and check every 7 minutes or so, until desired temperature is reached, about 2½ hours in all. The small end will register the highest temperature, and if you want some meat medium rare and the rest very rare, roast to 120°. Keeping the roast warm until serving time: If you know your oven is absolutely accurate and that you can keep it at around 115°, turn it off, remove the roast, leave the door open to cool oven for 15 minutes, then set thermostat at 115° and return roast to oven. For the "jus" (sauce), remove beef from roasting pan. Pour off accumulated fat, pour in the beef stock, and stir with a wooden spoon. Pour the liquid and roasting vegetables from the pan into a saucepan and simmer, mashing the vegetables into the liquid. Season carefully to taste, and skim off fat. Just before serving, strain into a hot sauce bowl.

Hint: A 5-rib roast takes approximately 2½ hours to cook, so start it 3 to 3½ hours before planning to serve.

Yield: 6 servings.

EASY CHATEAU STROGANOFF

1½ pounds beef tenderloin, cubed
1 onion, diced
8 ounces fresh mushrooms, sliced
1 small clove garlic, minced
2 (10¾ ounce) cans cream of mushroom soup, undiluted
2 teaspoons Dijon mustard
½ (10¾ ounce) can beef broth
¼ cup sherry
Flour
Salt
Pepper
Margarine
8 ounces sour cream
16 ounces egg noodles

Prepare beef by trimming fat, season with salt and pepper, and roll in flour. In one skillet, cook onions till tender. Add garlic and mushrooms and cook over medium heat for 2 or 3 minutes. Set aside. In separate large skillet, brown meat in 2 tablespoons margarine. Add onion, mushroom, and garlic mixture. Add mushroom soup, broth, and mustard. Heat to boiling. Reduce heat, cover and simmer for one hour, stirring occasionally. Add sherry and cook for another 20 to 30 minutes. Prepare noodles according to package directions. Stir sour cream into beef mixture and remove from heat. Ladle over noodles and serve.

Yield: 2 to 4 servings.

FILET MIGNON

1 tablespoon chopped fresh rosemary
1 teaspoon salt
1 teaspoon freshly ground pepper
1 clove garlic, minced
1 tablespoon grated lemon zest
4 filet mignon steaks, 2 to 3 inches thick
1½ tablespoons olive oil, divided
2 chopped green onions
1 red bell pepper, julienned
1 cup chicken stock
2 teaspoons fresh lemon juice
2 tablespoons unsalted butter

Combine rosemary, salt, pepper, garlic and zest. Rub steaks with ½ tablespoon olive oil and herb mixture. Sauté in remaining olive oil. Cook about 3 minutes per side. Remove when done to your preference. Add green onions and red pepper and cook 2 minutes. Stir in chicken stock and lemon juice. Reduce sauce by half. Stir in butter as desired to taste. Serve sauce over filets.

Yield: 4 servings.

GREAT BRISKET

1 (5 to 6 pound) brisket
1 (12 ounce) can cola-flavored carbonated beverage
1 (12 ounce) bottle chili sauce
1 envelope onion soup mix

Mix cola, chili sauce, and onion soup mix. Place brisket, fat side up, in a Dutch oven or 13 X 9 X 2 inch baking dish. Pour liquid mixture over brisket and cover tightly with lid or aluminum foil. Bake at 325° for 30 minutes per pound, about 3 hours, or until tender. Trim fat after cooking. Also can be cooked all day in a 220° oven.

Yield: 6 to 8 servings.

TERIYAKI

½ **cup soy sauce**
½ **cup sake or cooking sherry**
1 **clove garlic, minced**
2 **tablespoons fresh ginger, minced**
½ **cup green onions, finely sliced**
¼-½ **cup brown sugar or honey**
½ **teaspoon black pepper**
2 **teaspoons or more arrowroot for thickening marinade**
2 **(16 ounce) prime New York strip steaks**

Place meat in glass dish. Stir all ingredients together, except arrowroot, and simmer in a saucepan for 10 minutes. Do not boil. Reserve 1 cup for sauce. Pour marinade over meat and refrigerate for 8 hours. Charcoal broil meat or cook in oven under broiler to doneness desired. In saucepan, pour reserved sauce and add arrowroot. Stir until thick. Heat thoroughly and pour immediately onto meat and serve.

Yield: 4 servings.

BOB'S NEW YORK CORNED BEEF

1 **large pickled brisket in cryovac package**
4 **whole garlic heads cut in half, do not peel**
Paprika

Bring a very large pot of water to a rolling boil. Add brisket to boiling water and bring back to boiling. Add garlic. Cover and reduce heat. Simmer approximately 2 hours or just until tender. Do not overcook. Take large pan of ice and water and submerge hot brisket in it for 5 minutes. Remove from water. Trim fat and rub paprika on top. Slice thin for sandwiches.

Yield: 8 to 10 servings.

FLAMBÉED PEPPER STEAK

4 beef tenderloin or sirloin steaks
4 teaspoons green peppercorns
1 small onion
1 tablespoon butter
1 teaspoon salt
⅔ cup whipping cream
3 tablespoons beef stock
3 tablespoons cognac or brandy

Crush green peppercorns in mortar with pestle. Chop onion. Combine. Press peppercorn mixture into meat on both sides. In a skillet, heat butter until lightly browned. Add steaks. Brown well on one side. Turn steak over, brown on other side. Sprinkle lightly with salt. Remove steaks to a covered serving dish and keep warm. Add beef stock. Scrape up brown bits. Cook until reduced. Add cream, reduce slightly. Strain liquid. Set aside. Rinse skillet and heat again. Add steaks, pour cognac over. Ignite. Add cream mixture. Let cook for 1 to 2 minutes. Serve.

Hint: For best flavor, do not add cognac and ignite until steaks are ready to be served.

Yield: 4 servings.

KATHRYN'S STEW

4 pounds stew meat
½ cup red wine
1 (10¾ ounce) can mushroom soup
1 package onion soup mix
8 ounces fresh mushrooms

Mix wine, mushroom soup (with ½ can water added), onion soup mix and mushrooms. Mix well and pour over meat. Put in roaster, covered. Bake at 250° for 4 hours. Do not take cover off while baking. Serve over rice or noodles.

Yield: 10 to 12 servings.

TEXAS STEW

2 pounds ground beef
4 cloves garlic, minced
2 tablespoons margarine
2 (8 ounce) cans tomato sauce
Salt and pepper to taste
1 (8 ounce) package cream cheese, softened
6 green onions, chopped
1 small carton sour cream
1 (10 ounce) package small noodles, cooked and drained
2 cups diced cheddar cheese
1 (4½ ounce) can mushrooms, drained

Sauté beef and garlic in margarine until browned. Add tomato sauce. Combine cream cheese, onions and sour cream. Alternate layers of noodles, beef mixture, and cream cheese mixture twice in a large buttered casserole. Top with cheddar cheese, then with mushrooms. Bake at 350° for 30 minutes. Can be frozen.

Yield: 10 to 12 servings.

OVEN BEEF STEW

1-1½ pounds stew meat
Salt and pepper to taste
4-5 carrots
3-4 potatoes
2-3 celery stalks
4 garlic cloves, chopped
1 envelope onion soup mix
2 tablespoons tapioca flour
2½ cups water
1 cup tomato juice or tomato vegetable juice cocktail

Brown stew meat in large Dutch oven. Add remaining ingredients. Bake for 2½ to 3 hours at 275°.

Yield: 6 servings.

CHILI

2 pounds stew meat
1 pound ground meat
1 (8 ounce) can tomato sauce
16 ounces water
5 tablespoons ground chile pepper
1 tablespoon cumin
1 tablespoon oregano
1 teaspoon salt
2 tablespoons chopped onion
¼ teaspoon garlic
¼ teaspoon paprika
2½ tablespoons masa flour
Cayenne pepper to taste

Brown together stew meat and ground meat. Add tomato sauce, water and remaining ingredients, except the masa flour. Cook for 1 hour and 15 minutes or until meat is tender. Stir occasionally. Mix masa flour with warm water until slightly thickened and stir into chili. Let simmer another 15 to 20 minutes, then taste for tenderness and seasoning. Add as much cayenne pepper as you can stand.

Yield: 4 servings.

PETER MARZIO'S FAMOUS LASAGNA

10 Italian plum tomatoes
10 regular tomatoes
Kosher salt
Pepper
Fresh oregano
Olive oil
2 pounds lasagna noodles
½-1 pint heavy cream
1 quart ricotta cheese
1 pound mozzarella cheese
1 pound provolone cheese
Grated Parmesan cheese

Parboil the tomatoes until skins can be removed easily. Peel and seed tomatoes and place tomatoes in large bowl. Salt and pepper to taste. Add 2 tablespoons fresh oregano and mix. In a large saucepan, place 3 tablespoons of olive oil. Add tomato mixture and cook over low heat for 40 minutes. Do not cover. Boil water in large pasta pot. Add salt and olive oil to taste. When water is boiling, add the lasagna noodles. Cook until the pasta is limp but firm. Drain the water from the pot and add cold water. Drain again. In a large bowl, empty the ricotta cheese and fold in the cream. Add enough cream to enrich the ricotta without making it too thin or runny. In a large rectangular baking dish, place two tablespoons of olive oil, a pinch of salt and some oregano. Cover the bottom of the dish with lasagna noodles. Add thin layers of tomato sauce, ricotta/cream mixture, mozzarella, Parmesan, tomato sauce again and finally provolone cheese. Add a second layer of pasta and repeat the layers. Continue this process until baking dish is ⅘ filled. End with a layer of pasta and cover with a thin layer of tomato sauce. Bake at 350° covered for one hour. Uncover and bake for 10 minutes more. Remove from oven. Let cool 5 minutes. Cut into squares. Add Parmesan cheese and heated tomato sauce to taste.

Variation: Add sausage, chopped meat, onions, or peppers to tomato sauce.

Yield: 12 servings.

BEEF AND CHEDDAR LOAF

1½ pounds ground beef
¾ cup bread crumbs
½ cup coarsely shredded sharp cheddar cheese
¼ cup minced onion
1 teaspoon salt
¼ teaspoon pepper
½ teaspoon dry mustard
1 egg, slightly beaten
¾ cup milk

Combine all ingredients in a large bowl. Mix well. Pack firmly into an 8 X 4 inch loaf pan. Bake at 350° for 1 hour and 15 minutes. Let stand 5 minutes. Slice and serve.

Hint: The use of sharp cheddar cheese is crucial to the overall taste.

Yield: 4 to 6 servings.

MOIST MEAT LOAF

1 pound lean ground beef
1 egg
1 medium can tomato wedges, reserve liquid
2-3 tablespoons dry onion soup mix
Salt and pepper to taste
¼ cup green bell pepper, optional
¼ cup mushrooms, optional
1-2 slices bread

In a large bowl, mix beef, egg, drained tomatoes, soup mix, salt, pepper, and green pepper and mushrooms, if desired. Add bread, which has been soaked in the tomato liquid. Mix thoroughly. Place in loaf pan and bake at 350° for approximately 1 hour. Check and drain liquid, if any, after 40 minutes. Reserve liquid for gravy base.

Variation: Can substitute ½ cup finely chopped onion for dry onion soup mix.

Yield: 6 servings.

EGGPLANT MOUSSAKA

½ **cup butter or vegetable oil, divided**
1½ **pounds ground meat**
2 **tablespoons chopped onion**
½ **cup white wine**
1½ **pounds ripe tomatoes, peeled and drained**
2 **tablespoons chopped parsley**
Salt and pepper to taste
3 **pounds eggplant**
Oil for frying
1 **recipe Béchamel Sauce (recipe follows)**
1 **cup bread crumbs**
½ **cup grated Parmesan cheese**
2-3 **tablespoons melted butter**
½ **teaspoon cinnamon, optional**

Place half the butter (or oil) in a frying pan. Add ground meat and onions. Stir to crumble the meat and cook until browned. Add wine, tomatoes, parsley, salt and pepper, and bring to a boil. Lower the heat until the liquids are absorbed. Wash and dry the eggplant. Cut into thin slices. Fry in the remaining butter (or oil). Place the fried eggplant slices on a platter. Prepare the Béchamel sauce. Arrange half of the eggplant slices in even rows in a medium sized baking pan. Sprinkle with half the breadcrumbs. Add half the cheese to the ground meat, and mix it well. Spread this on top of the eggplant. Add another layer of eggplant, then cover with the Béchamel sauce. Sprinkle the remaining cheese on top, then the remaining breadcrumbs. Drizzle some melted butter on top. Bake in a preheated 325° oven for 35 to 40 minutes until lightly browned.

Yield: 8 servings.

BÉCHAMEL SAUCE

6 tablespoons butter
7-8 tablespoons flour
4 cups milk, scalded
1-2 egg yolks
Salt and pepper to taste
½ teaspoon nutmeg (optional)

Melt the butter, but do not brown. Add the flour slowly, stirring constantly. Remove from heat, and slowly pour in the milk. Return to heat and continue stirring until the sauce thickens. Beat the egg yolks well, and add them to mixture. Add salt and pepper to taste. Add nutmeg, if desired. Continue stirring until well blended.

MACARONI PASTITSIO WITH PHYLLO PASTRY (PASTILLA)

1½ pounds thick macaroni
1 cup butter
2 eggs
¼-½ pound Parmesan cheese, grated
1¾ pounds chopped meat or ground beef
1 medium onion, chopped
½ cup white wine
1½ pounds ripe tomatoes, peeled and drained
Salt and pepper to taste
1 piece of stick cinnamon
Pinch of ground nutmeg, optional
¾ pound phyllo pastry
Butter for brushing the phyllo

Cook the macaroni in salted water, drain. Melt ⅓ cup butter and pour over the macaroni. Beat the eggs lightly and mix them with the macaroni. Sprinkle with half the cheese. Brown the remaining butter, chopped meat, and onion in a large pot. Stir the chopped meat to break it up. Add the wine, tomatoes, salt, pepper and cinnamon. Butter a deep pan. Layer with 6 to 8 sheets of phyllo, and allow the sides to overlap the pan, brushing each phyllo with melted butter. Divide the macaroni into three portions and the meat into two. Put one layer of macaroni on the phyllo, alternating with the meat until you top it off with the macaroni. Fold the overlapping phyllo over the filling and brush with butter. Top with the remaining phyllo, brushing each sheet with butter. Trim the excess with a sharp knife. Brush the top phyllo with butter. Bake in a preheated 350° oven for 30 minutes or until golden brown. Remove from the oven, and cut in small rectangles.

Variation: You can replace the tomatoes with 1 tablespoon tomato paste diluted with a cup of water.

Variation: You can replace the phyllo pastry with Béchamel sauce.

Yield: 8 to 10 servings.

SWEET AND SOUR CABBAGE ROLLS

1 head leafy green cabbage
1½ pounds lean ground beef
1 egg
½ grated onion
1 whole onion, chopped
¼ cup cracker meal
Salt and pepper
2 tablespoons oil
1 (15 ounce) can tomato sauce
6 tablespoons brown sugar
2 tablespoons vinegar

Put cabbage in a large pot of water to half cover and heat on medium until slightly softened (approximately 10 minutes). Turn over so other side can soften for another 10 minutes. When done, remove from water and put in colander to drain and cool. Meanwhile, mix meat, egg, grated onion, cracker meal, salt and pepper. Form into meatballs about the size of a walnut. Core the cabbage and gently pull off as many softened leaves as possible. Roll one meatball in each leaf, tucking ends in, until all softened leaves are used up. Chop up the remaining cabbage. In large roasting pan, sauté chopped onion and leftover cabbage in oil along with a few loose pieces of ground meat. When softened, lay cabbage rolls on top along with any extra meatballs not in cabbage leaves. Pour can of tomato sauce evenly over meatballs and then add ½ can water. Sprinkle the brown sugar evenly over the rolls and then the vinegar. Cover and bake at 325° for one hour. Remove from oven and turn cabbage rolls and meatballs over. Bake for one more hour at 325° uncovered. Serve with rice.

Yield: 6 servings.

VEAL CUTLETS PARMESAN

1 pound veal cutlets, cut into ¼-inch slices
3 tablespoons grated Parmesan cheese
½ cup Italian bread crumbs
1 egg
2 tablespoons water
¼ cup olive oil
Salt and pepper to taste
4 onions, thinly sliced
2 cloves garlic, minced
8 tablespoons olive oil
2 teaspoons basil
12 ounces tomato paste diluted with 2 cans water
½ teaspoon sugar
½ pound mozzarella cheese slices

Mix Parmesan cheese and bread crumbs. Mix egg and water. Dip meat into egg, then crumbs. Cook in ¼-cup olive oil for about 5 minutes on each side until golden brown. Place browned cutlets in baking dish. Make a tomato sauce by cooking garlic and onion in oil for about 10 minutes. Add basil then remaining ingredients (except cheese slices) and simmer for 30 minutes. Pour most of tomato sauce over veal cutlets. Place cheese slices on top and pour rest of sauce over cheese. Bake at 325° for 25 minutes.

Yield: 4 servings.

ZURICH GESCHNETZELTES (VEAL)

21 ounces veal (loin or filet), thinly sliced
2 tablespoons butter
Salt and pepper
1 onion, finely chopped
½ cup sliced mushrooms
¾ cup white wine
¾ cup cream
Few drops of lemon juice
1 tablespoon chopped parsley

Sauté the thinly sliced veal on each side in very hot butter. Remove from pan, sprinkle with salt and pepper and keep warm. Slightly reduce the heat and add onion to the butter and juice from the meat. Add mushrooms. Sauté briefly then pour in the wine. Simmer until the liquid is reduced by half. Add the cream and bring to a boil, then add salt, pepper and lemon juice. Reheat the meat in the sauce, but do not let it boil. Serve topped with parsley.

Variations: Can use chicken breasts or veal kidneys instead of veal.

Yield: 6 servings.

GRILLADES

4 pounds beef or veal round roast, sliced ½-inch thick
½ cup bacon drippings
½ cup flour
1 cup chopped onion
2 cups chopped green onions
¾ cup chopped celery
1½ cups chopped green bell pepper
2 cloves garlic, minced
2 cups chopped tomatoes
½ teaspoon tarragon, optional
⅔ teaspoon thyme
1 cup water
1 cup red wine
3 teaspoons salt
½ teaspoon black pepper
2 bay leaves
½ teaspoon red pepper sauce
2 tablespoons Worcestershire sauce
3 tablespoons chopped parsley

Remove fat from meat. Cut meat into serving-size pieces. Pound to ¼-inch thick. In a Dutch oven, brown meat well in 4 tablespoons bacon drippings. Remove to warm plate. To Dutch oven, add 4 tablespoons bacon drippings and flour. Stir and cook to make a dark brown roux. Add onion, green onions, celery, green pepper, and garlic, and sauté until limp. Add tomatoes, tarragon, and thyme, and cook 3 minutes. Add water and wine. Stir well for several minutes, return meat, add salt, pepper, bay leaves, hot pepper sauce, and Worcestershire. Lower heat, stir, and continue cooking. If veal round is used, simmer covered approximately 1 hour. If beef round is used, simmer covered approximately 2 hours. Remove bay leaves. Stir in parsley. More liquid may be added. Serve with rice or grits.

Hint: Best if prepared the day before serving. Traditionally served for breakfast or brunch.

Yield: 6 to 8 servings.

SPICY BRAISED PORK

⅓ **cup flour**
1 **tablespoon ground coriander**
2 **teaspoons ground turmeric**
2 **teaspoons ground cumin**
1 **teaspoon ground paprika**
1 **teaspoon ground cayenne pepper**
1½ **pounds diced pork**
2 **tablespoons oil**
2 **onions, thinly sliced**
4 **dried curry leaves (available in Indian markets)**
1 **teaspoon grated fresh ginger, optional**
2½ **cups chicken stock**
⅓ **cup fruit chutney**

Combine the flour, coriander, turmeric, cumin, paprika and cayenne pepper in a bowl. Add the pork and stir until it is well coated with spices. Heat oil in a large pan, add onions, curry leaves, and ginger, if desired. Stir over medium heat for 3 minutes or until tender. Remove from the pan. Add the pork to the pan, cook over medium high heat for 3 minutes or until browned, turning occasionally. Return the onion mixture to the pan with the stock and chutney. Bring to a boil, reduce heat to low, cover and simmer for 30 to 40 minutes or until the pork is tender. Serve with rice or noodles.

Hint: If you don't have any fruit chutney, you can use stewed apples.

Yield: 4 servings.

TWICE-COOKED PORK WITH CABBAGE AND SAI FUN

½ pound yam noodles (cellophane or bean thread noodles)
3 tablespoons sesame oil
3 tablespoons chili paste with garlic
4 garlic cloves, minced
2 cups cooked pork, cut into ¼-inch pieces
1 onion, chopped
1 green bell pepper, chopped
1 red bell pepper, chopped
1 cup broccoli florets
4 cups chopped bok choy
Japanese forest mushrooms (oyster or wood ear)
3 tablespoons soy sauce
16 scallions
Splash rice wine

Soak noodles in a small bowl for 30 minutes. Heat sesame oil in wok. Add chili paste and garlic and cook for a minute. Add pork, onion, peppers, broccoli and cook for two minutes. Add noodles, bok choy, and mushrooms. Stir in soy sauce and rice wine. Sprinkle with scallions. Serve over rice.

Yield: 8 servings.

MARINATED PORK TENDERLOIN

1 **pork tenderloin (1 pound)**
2 **tablespoons soy sauce**
2 **tablespoons dry sherry**
2 **garlic cloves, crushed**
2 **teaspoons grated peeled ginger root**
3 **small zucchini (8 ounces each)**
2 **green onions**
1 **large red bell pepper**
1 **tablespoon olive oil**
½ **teaspoon salt**
1¾ **teaspoons sugar**
½ **teaspoon cornstarch**

Trim any excess fat from pork tenderloin. In 11 X 7 inch glass baking dish, mix soy sauce, sherry, garlic and ginger root. Add tenderloin. Cover and refrigerate, turning tenderloin occasionally, about 40 minutes. While tenderloin is marinating, cut zucchini into bite size chunks. Cut green onions into 2-inch long pieces and then thinly slice lengthwise. Cut red pepper into 2-inch long strips. About 20 minutes before serving, preheat broiler and place tenderloin on rack in broiling pan; reserve marinade. With broiling pan 5 to 7 inches from source of heat, broil tenderloin for 12 to 15 minutes, turning once until it is browned on the outside and still slightly pink in the center (160°). Meanwhile, in non-stick 10-inch skillet over medium heat, in hot olive oil, cook zucchini, green onions and red pepper until vegetables are crisp. Salt to taste. Pour reserved marinade into small saucepan. Over medium heat, heat marinade and sugar to boiling. In a cup mix cornstarch and ½ cup cold water until blended. Stir into mixture in saucepan. Heat sauce to boiling. Boil 1 minute. Place tenderloin on cutting board, let stand 5 minutes, cut into ½-inch thick slices. Arrange pork and vegetables on large warm platter. Spoon sauce over pork.

Yield: 4 servings.

PORK TENDERLOIN MEDALLIONS

- ⅓ cup Dijon mustard
- 2 tablespoons vegetable oil
- 1 teaspoon dried tarragon, crumbled
- 2 pork tenderloins, cut across grain into 1-inch thick slices
- ½ cup whole wheat flour
- ½ cup seasoned breadcrumbs
- Cracked pepper to taste
- 3 tablespoons vegetable oil
- 1 cup white wine

Combine mustard, 2 tablespoons oil, and tarragon. Spread generously on pork slices. Refrigerate at least 2 hours (can be prepared a day ahead). Cover pork loosely. Combine flour, pepper, and breadcrumbs. Dip pork into mixture, coating generously. Heat 3 tablespoons oil in large skillet over medium-high heat. Add pork, brown on one side about 4 minutes. Turn and brown second side. Add wine, cover and cook five more minutes. Serve with sauce over.

Yield: 2 servings.

RON'S PORK CHOPS

- Boneless pork loin chops (1 per person)
- Fresh rosemary
- Salt and freshly ground pepper to taste
- Olive oil
- Apple cider

For each serving, pat pork chop with chopped rosemary to almost completely coat. Season with salt and pepper to taste. Brown both sides of pork chop in skillet with olive oil. Pour enough apple cider into skillet to cover pork chops. Cover and cook on low heat until done (approximately 45 to 50 minutes). Remove pork chops to serving plate. Scrape and reduce pan drippings.

Yield: You decide!

PORK TENDERLOIN WITH APPLE AND RED CHILE CHUTNEY

4 pork loin chops, 6 to 8 ounces each
2 cups apple cider
3 tablespoons light brown sugar
2 tablespoons chili powder

Apple and Red Chili Chutney

4 Granny Smith apples, peeled, cored and coarsely chopped
4 fresh red chiles, diced
½ cup brown sugar
⅓ cup cider vinegar
1 cup water
1 tablespoon chopped fresh marjoram
½ cup roasted pine nuts, optional

To prepare the chutney, place apples and chiles in a heavy stainless steel saucepan with sugar, vinegar, garlic, and water. Cook until apples are tender. Stir in marjoram and add pine nuts, if desired. Allow to cool and refrigerate. Best if prepared the day before serving.

Pork Marinade

½ cup sugar
1½ tablespoons salt
1 tablespoon thyme
½ tablespoon ground cumin
1 tablespoon crushed bay leaf
1 teaspoon crushed black pepper
1 teaspoon oregano
3 tablespoons chili caribe
4 allspice berries
4 cloves
1 stick cinnamon
6 cups water

Mix the marinade ingredients together, add the pork and marinate overnight.

Remove pork and bring to room temperature. Combine apple cider, brown sugar, and chili powder. Grill meat over a hot fire for 7 to 10 minutes, or broil until internal temperature reaches 140°. Baste with a little apple cider mixture as meat cooks. Serve pork with chutney.

Yield: 8 to 12 servings.

GOURMET PORK FILET

2 pork tenderloins
Salt and pepper
Paprika
Bacon
2 teaspoons butter
1 onion, chopped
1 clove garlic, minced
3 tablespoons parsley, chopped
12-16 ounces mushrooms, sliced
1 teaspoon rosemary
1 tablespoon fresh sage, chopped or 1 teaspoon dried sage
1 teaspoon marjoram
White wine
¾ cup heavy cream
3 teaspoons corn starch

Cut pork tenderloin in 2-inch long pieces. Season well with salt, pepper and paprika. Wrap bacon strip around each piece of pork filet and secure with toothpicks. Set aside. In a heavy skillet, sauté onions, garlic, parsley, mushrooms and all of the spices in the butter. Pour into a buttered casserole dish. Add tenderloin pieces and dot with a small piece of butter. Add white wine ¼-inch deep to the casserole. Bake for 20 minutes at 400°. Add ¾ cup heavy cream mixed with 3 teaspoons cornstarch and bake for 15 minutes longer at 375°.

Yield: 6 to 8 servings.

LAMB SHANKS À LA MERRILY

4 lamb shanks (3¼-4 pounds)
4 onions, thinly sliced
¾ cup dry vermouth
Splash of rice wine
¼ cup lemon juice
¼ cup soy sauce
4 cloves garlic
Pepper to taste

Arrange onion slices in ovenproof pan. Top with lamb shanks and pour vermouth over. Stir together lemon juice, soy sauce, garlic, pepper, to taste, and rice wine and pour over shanks. Bake at 350° for 3½ to 4 hours, or until lamb is done. Remove lamb and onions to serving platter. Skim and discard fat from pan juices. Reduce juices on high heat until about ¼ cup remains. Serve onions and shanks with rice, and spoon juices over all.

Yield: 4 servings.

LAMB AND WHITE BEAN RAGOÛT

1½ cups northern beans
Salt
1 lamb shoulder (6-7 pounds) trimmed and boned
8 garlic cloves, crushed
1 cup red wine vinegar
½ cup olive oil
1 teaspoon thyme
1 teaspoon marjoram
2 medium onions, chopped
5 sliced carrots
1 (35 ounce) can plum tomatoes, drained
¼ cup flour
2 cups beef stock
1 teaspoon basil
2 bay leaves

Rinse beans. Place beans in large pot, cover with cold water and let stand overnight. Drain. Add cold water to cover by 3 inches. Bring to boil and simmer partially covered until beans are almost tender, about 1 hour. Stir in 1 teaspoon salt and cook for 15 to 20 minutes. Drain. Cut lamb into 1-inch cubes. Add garlic, red wine vinegar and herbs. Let marinate overnight. Heat oven to 350°. Remove lamb from marinade and reserve liquid. Pat dry. Heat 3 tablespoons olive oil in a Dutch oven. Sear lamb over high heat until brown. Add oil as needed. Add 1 tablespoon oil, lower heat, and add onions. Cover and cook until tender. Remove from pan. Stir in flour and cook 3 minutes. Whisk in reserved marinade and beef stock. Add drained tomatoes and 2 teaspoons salt. Bring to a boil. Return meat to kettle with any accumulated juices, cover and bake for 1 hour. Stir in carrots and bake 30 minutes. Stir in beans and bake until ragoût thickens, about 15 minutes. Season with pepper.

Yield: 8 servings.

POULTRY & SEAFOOD COLLECTION

Edouard Manet, French, 1832-1883
The Toilers of the Sea, 1873
Oil on canvas, 25 x 31¼ in.
The Museum of Fine Arts, Houston, gift of Audrey Jones Beck

Manet frequently revisited the seaside for inspiration for works that run the spectrum from the elegant Parisian at the beach for leisure to those who toiled there. As a man of privilege and education from a well-to-do family, Manet frequently defied conventional style to set the avant-garde pace for his time. In this painting he successfully makes a bridge from the Realist School to that which will become the Impressionists (though he would never agree to exhibit with them). The brushstrokes become a part of the subject as long as fluid strokes create a folded mast, broad patches of color become coats and sea spray, and carefully modeled smaller strokes detail the man and his bait on the right.

Poultry & Seafood Collection

Mary Anne Varner's Rococo Chicken
Chicken with Artichokes
Chicken Breast in Rum Sauce
Chicken Pillows for Two
Muenster Chicken
Creamy Baked Chicken Breasts
Chicken Enchiladas
Almond Poppy Chicken
Chicken Curry
Hawaiian Chicken Curry
Poached Chicken with Black Beans and Salsa
Savory Chicken and Asparagus
Creamy Chicken
Chicken Fricassee
Chicken Sauté with Fresh Ginger
Mole de Pollo – Chicken with Peanut Butter Sauce
Soft Chicken Tacos
Csirke Paprikas Budapest (Chicken Paprika)
Canard L'Orange (Roast Duck with Oranges)
Glazed Cornish Hens with Curried Rice
Moules Mariniere (Mussels in white wine)
Alison's Salmon
Salmon Soufflé
Truites a' l'Ardennaise
Salmon with Cucumber Sauce
Peppery Garlic Shrimp with Sherry Sauce
Shrimp Annie
Gambas al Ajillo
David's BBQ Shrimp

MARY ANNE VARNER'S ROCOCO CHICKEN

10 ounces sharp cheddar cheese (block)
4 chicken breasts, boned and skinned
2 eggs, beaten
¾ cup dry breadcrumbs
Margarine for browning
1 chicken bouillon cube
1 cup boiling water
½ cup chopped onion
½ cup chopped green bell pepper
⅓ cup margarine
2 tablespoons flour
1 teaspoon salt
½ teaspoon pepper
2 cups cooked white rice
1 cup cooked wild rice
1 (3 ounce) can sliced mushrooms, drained

Heat oven to 400°. Cut cheese in 8 equal sticks. Cut chicken breasts in half and flatten to ¼-inch thickness. Roll each piece around a stick of cheese; secure with toothpicks. Dip in eggs, then in breadcrumbs and brown in margarine. Dissolve bouillon cube in water. Cook onion and green pepper in ⅓ cup margarine until tender. Add flour, seasonings, and bouillon. Cook until thickened. Add rice and mushrooms, pour into a 10 X 8 inch baking dish. Top with chicken and bake for 20 minutes.

Yield: 4 servings.

CHICKEN WITH ARTICHOKES

8 boneless, skinless chicken breasts
Paprika
Salt and pepper
¼ pound butter
1 (15 ounce) can artichoke hearts
½ pound fresh sliced mushrooms
3 tablespoons flour
⅓ cup sherry
1½ cups chicken stock

Season chicken with salt and pepper then sprinkle liberally with paprika. Sauté breasts in half of the butter until brown. Place chicken pieces and artichoke hearts in large serving casserole. Put mushrooms and remaining butter in same skillet and sauté for about 5 minutes. Sprinkle flour in gently and add sherry and chicken stock. Simmer 5 to 10 minutes more, stirring constantly, or until thickened and pour over chicken and artichokes. Cover and bake at 375° for 1 hour.

Yield: 8 servings.

CHICKEN BREAST IN RUM SAUCE

1½ pounds boneless chicken breasts
Salt and pepper to taste
3 tablespoons butter or margarine, divided
2 tablespoons finely chopped green onion
¼ pound mushrooms, quartered
3 tablespoons dark rum (80 proof)
1½ cups heavy cream

Flour and cook chicken until done and brown in 2 tablespoons of butter and set aside. Melt remaining tablespoon butter in skillet. Add onion and mushrooms and cook briefly. Sprinkle with rum. Add cream and reduce over high heat about 5 minutes. Add salt and pepper to taste. Pour sauce over chicken and serve with rice.

Yield: 4 servings.

CHICKEN PILLOWS FOR TWO

1 whole chicken breast, halved, skinned and boned
1 clove garlic
2 slices (1 ounce) prosciutto or boiled ham
2 slices (1 ounce) mozzarella cheese, thinly sliced
2 tablespoons seasoned breadcrumbs
2 tablespoons medium dry sherry
2 tablespoons clarified butter
Salt and freshly ground pepper to taste
1 tablespoon chopped parsley

Pound chicken breast pieces to a thickness of ¼-inch. Rub each chicken breast piece with cut garlic cloves. Place prosciutto and cheese over chicken. Sprinkle with breadcrumbs. Roll up, starting at broad end, and secure with wooden picks. Place in a lightly greased shallow baking dish. Combine sherry and clarified butter, heat briefly. Pour over chicken and season with salt and pepper. Bake at 350° for 20 to 25 minutes or until chicken is done. Sprinkle with parsley.

Hint: To clarify butter, melt butter over low heat in a heavy saucepan, without stirring. When completely melted, remove from heat and skim any foam from top. Slowly pour the clear layer into a dish, reserving the milky layer in pan. Discard milk solids.

Yield: 2 servings.

MUENSTER CHICKEN

4 whole boneless chicken breasts
3 eggs
Italian breadcrumbs
1 pound mushrooms, sliced
¾ cup beef broth
⅓ pound Muenster cheese, grated

Cut chicken into bite sized pieces. Soak in slightly beaten egg for 2 hours in refrigerator. Dip in Italian breadcrumbs. Sauté lightly in margarine until lightly browned. Place in casserole dish. Sauté sliced mushrooms until tender. Place over chicken. Pour beef broth over chicken, cover with Muenster cheese. Bake 30 minutes uncovered.

Yield: 4 to 6 servings.

CREAMY BAKED CHICKEN BREASTS

4 whole chicken breasts, split, skinned and boned
8 (4 X 4 inch) Swiss cheese slices
1 (10¾ ounce) can cream of chicken soup, undiluted
¼ cup dry white wine
1 cup herb seasoned stuffing mix, crushed
¼ cup melted butter or margarine

Lightly grease a 13 X 9 X 2 inch baking dish. Arrange chicken in pan and top with cheese slices. Combine soup and wine, stirring well. Spoon sauce over chicken evenly. Sprinkle stuffing mix over sauce and drizzle butter over the top. Bake at 350° for 50 to 60 minutes.

Yield: 4 servings.

CHICKEN ENCHILADAS

1 whole chicken, poached
2 (4 ounce) cans green chiles
1 (16 ounce) container sour cream
2 (10¾ ounce) cans cream of chicken soup, undiluted
2 packages flour tortillas
2 cups grated sharp cheddar cheese
1-2 cups mozzarella cheese
1-2 cups Monterey Jack cheese
Black olives, optional

Bone chicken and tear or cut into bite sized pieces. Mix green chiles, sour cream and soup together. Spread small amount of sour cream mixture over tortillas, then add small amount of chicken, cheese, and black olives, if desired. Roll and place in greased 13 X 9 X 2 inch casserole. Add remaining sour cream mixture and extra cheese. Bake at 350° for 30 minutes.

Yield: 20 enchiladas.

ALMOND POPPY CHICKEN

8 chicken breasts, poached, skinned and boned, cut into chunks
1 (8 ounce) container sour cream
1 (10¾ ounce) can cream of chicken soup, undiluted
White sauce (recipe below)
1 cup sautéed celery
1 cup sautéed mushrooms
1 stack round buttery crackers
2 tablespoons poppy seeds
½ cup sliced almonds
4 ounces butter

Mix chicken chunks, sour cream, chicken soup, white sauce, celery, and mushrooms and put into a buttered 9 X 13 X 2 inch casserole dish. Crush crackers in a plastic bag. Add poppy seeds and almonds. Shake bag well. Melt butter and add cracker mixture to it. Pour over chicken mixture. Bake 30 to 40 minutes at 350°.

White Sauce

2 tablespoons butter
2 tablespoons flour
¼ teaspoon salt
1 cup milk

Melt butter. Remove from heat. Add flour and salt. Add milk a little bit at a time, stirring until thickened.

Yield: 8 servings.

CHICKEN CURRY

- **6** **cloves garlic or ¾ teaspoon minced garlic**
- **¾** **teaspoon minced ginger**
- **4** **dried red chiles**
- **1** **tablespoon coriander seeds**
- **1** **teaspoon cumin seeds**
- **10** **black peppercorns**
- **Cinnamon stick, 1-inch long**
- **¼** **fresh coconut grated or 2 tablespoons dehydrated coconut**
- **1** **whole chicken, cut into 8 pieces**
- **2** **onions, finely sliced**
- **2** **tablespoons poppy seeds**
- **2** **ounces cashews**
- **2** **ounces sultanas (Thompson seedless grapes)**
- **2** **teaspoons salt**
- **2** **cups coconut milk or 2 ounces cream of coconut with 2 cups water**
- **2** **tablespoons cream**
- **4** **tablespoons oil**

In food processor, grind first 8 ingredients to a paste. Grind poppy seeds, cashews, and sultanas each separately. In a pan, heat oil and sauté onion until brown. Add spice paste to onion and blend well. Cook at least 5 minutes adding a little water if paste gets too dry. Add ground poppy seeds, cashew nuts and sultanas. Cook 5 minutes more. Add pieces of chicken and fry chicken for 10 minutes in spice paste, stirring occasionally, and adding a little water if necessary. Add salt, coconut milk and 2 cups water, cover and cook on low heat until chicken is tender. If curry is too thick, add 1 or 2 cups water and continue simmering a few minutes longer. If more water is added, taste for salt and add more if necessary. Before serving, add cream and simmer 5 minutes. Serve with boiled white rice.

Yield: 4 servings.

HAWAIIAN CHICKEN CURRY

- 6 tablespoons butter
- 4 tablespoons onion, chopped
- 2 cloves garlic, minced
- 1 teaspoon minced fresh ginger or ¼ teaspoon powdered ginger
- 3-4 tablespoons curry powder, to taste
- 1-2 tablespoons sugar, divided
- Pinch of salt
- 4 cups chicken broth
- 2 teaspoons corn starch
- ¼ cup cold water
- 2-3 (14 ounce) cans pure coconut milk
- 1 apple, peeled, pared and chopped
- 5-6 cups cooked chicken, cubed

In melted butter, sauté onion, garlic, and ginger until onions are translucent. Stir in curry powder, 1 tablespoon sugar, and pinch of salt until smooth. Combine with chicken broth. Mix cornstarch and cold water. Slowly add cornstarch mixture to thicken a bit. Stir in coconut milk, check for taste (may need to add a bit more of sugar). Add chicken and apple. Simmer about 1 hour. Do not boil. Serve with fluffy white rice and 6 to 8 condiments from the list below. Always include the chutney.

List of Condiments: mango chutney, chopped banana, grated hard-boiled eggs, chopped green onion, coconut - shredded or toasted, chopped peanuts, raisins, chopped bacon, diced avocado, diced tomatoes, green or ripe olives, sliced.

Yield: 6 to 10 servings.

POACHED CHICKEN WITH BLACK BEANS AND SALSA

1 cup chicken broth
6 chicken breast halves, skinned and boned
¼ cup dry white wine
¼ teaspoon salt
¼ teaspoon pepper
1 (15 ounce) can black beans, undrained
2 teaspoons balsamic or red wine vinegar
Dash of red pepper
Salsa

SALSA

1 large tomato, diced
1 serrano or other hot green chile pepper, minced
1 small onion, diced
1 clove garlic, minced
½ cup cilantro or parsley, finely chopped
¼ teaspoon salt
⅓ teaspoon pepper

Prepare salsa first by combining ingredients and refrigerating 2 to 3 hours. Bring chicken broth to a boil in a large skillet. Add chicken, wine, salt and pepper. Cover and reduce heat. Simmer mixture 15 to 20 minutes. Remove from heat. Use an electric blender or food processor to process beans until smooth. Combine beans, vinegar, and red pepper in a saucepan. Heat thoroughly, stirring occasionally. Add 1 to 2 tablespoons broth from chicken if mixture is too thick. Divide bean mixture on individual serving plates. Drain chicken and arrange over bean purée. Top with salsa. Serve immediately.

Yield: 6 servings.

SAVORY CHICKEN AND ASPARAGUS

1½ pounds fresh asparagus
4 boneless, skinless chicken breast halves
2 tablespoons cooking oil
½ teaspoon salt
¼ teaspoon pepper
½ cup mayonnaise
1 (10¾ ounce) can condensed cream of chicken soup, undiluted
1 teaspoon lemon juice
½ teaspoon curry powder
1 cup shredded sharp cheddar cheese

Partially cook the asparagus and drain. Place in greased 9-inch square baking dish. In skillet over medium heat, brown the chicken on both sides in oil. Season with salt and pepper. Arrange over asparagus. Mix together mayonnaise, soup, lemon juice, and curry. Pour over chicken and asparagus. Cover and bake at 375° for 40 minutes. Sprinkle with grated cheese. Let stand 5 minutes before serving.

Yield: 4 servings.

CREAMY CHICKEN

8 chicken breasts, poached, boned
1 cup sour cream
1 cup chicken broth
1 (10¾ ounce) can cream of chicken soup
1 stack round buttery crackers, crushed
2 ounces butter, melted

Tear or chop chicken into bite sized pieces. Mix all ingredients (except crackers and butter). Pour into 2 quart baking dish. Sprinkle crumbs on top. Drizzle butter on top of crumbs. Bake at 350° for 35 minutes.

Hint: To poach chicken, put chicken in skillet and cover with water, white wine, parsley stems, thyme and white peppercorns. Add salt and pepper to taste. Gently simmer until done.

Yield: 6 servings.

CHICKEN FRICASSEE

1 (3 pound) chicken, cut up
3-4 cloves garlic
1 onion, chopped
1 bell pepper, chopped
1 bay leaf
1 whole lemon
1 teaspoon cumin
2 teaspoons salt, or to taste
¼ teaspoon freshly ground black pepper
¼ cup olive oil
1 pound potatoes, peeled and quartered
1 (8 ounce) can tomato sauce
¼ cup green olives
¼ teaspoon saffron
2½ cups water, or more as needed

Over medium heat, sauté chicken, garlic, onion, bell pepper, bay leaf, lemon juice, cumin, salt and pepper in olive oil. Cook for 15 to 20 minutes or until chicken is nearly done. Add potatoes, tomato sauce, olives and saffron with water. Cook another 15 minutes or until potatoes are tender and liquid is thickened. Serve over steamed rice.

Hint: Can substitute wine for water.

Yield: 4 servings.

CHICKEN SAUTÉ WITH FRESH GINGER

Cooking oil
1¼ pounds chicken, cut into 1-inch pieces
½ green bell pepper, sliced
½ red bell pepper, sliced
1 medium carrot, thinly sliced
1 leek, thinly sliced
2 cups bean sprouts
1 inch piece fresh ginger, peeled and thinly sliced
2 tablespoons soy sauce
4 teaspoons white wine vinegar
1 cup chicken stock
Fresh ground black pepper
Cooked white rice

Season chicken with pepper and sauté in oil for about 3 minutes, stirring frequently. Remove from pan and keep warm. Sauté pepper and carrot 2 minutes. Add leek and bean sprouts. Stir in ginger, soy sauce and vinegar. Add chicken and chicken stock and stir continuously until boiling.

Yield: 4 to 6 servings.

MOLE DE POLLO — CHICKEN WITH PEANUT BUTTER SAUCE

2½ pounds chicken
1 teaspoon garlic powder
½ teaspoon ground cumin
¾ cup creamy peanut butter
3 tablespoons chili powder
Salt and pepper to taste

Poach chicken in water with garlic, cumin, salt and pepper. Reserve broth. Bone chicken and place in a casserole dish. To 2½ cups broth from chicken, add chili powder and peanut butter. Simmer for 10 minutes, stirring often. Pour over chicken and cover. Bake at 350° for 25 minutes.

Yield: 4 to 6 servings.

SOFT CHICKEN TACOS

3 chicken breasts
1 medium onion, chopped
1 cup green bell pepper, chopped
1 clove garlic
Olive oil
1 (14 ounce) can tomatoes with diced chiles
1 (6 ounce) can tomato sauce
1 teaspoon cumin
1 teaspoon garlic powder
Salt and pepper to taste
12 flour tortillas
1 pint sour cream
1 cup grated Monterey Jack cheese

Cook chicken and chop into small pieces. In large skillet, sauté onion, bell pepper, and garlic in olive oil. Add tomatoes with chiles and tomato sauce. Add chicken and spices. Simmer. Warm tortillas. In each tortilla, place chicken mixture, sour cream, and grated cheese. Roll.

Yield: 4 servings.

CSIRKE PAPRIKAS BUDAPEST (CHICKEN PAPRIKA)

⅔ cup chopped Spanish onion
2 tablespoons vegetable oil
¼ cup sweet paprika
¾ cup canned chicken broth, divided
3½ pounds chicken, diced into ½-inch pieces
2 green bell peppers, cut into ½-inch pieces
3 tomatoes, cut into ½-inch pieces
½ cup sour cream
1 tablespoon all-purpose flour

In a Dutch oven, cook onion in oil over low heat until translucent. Remove from heat and stir in paprika and ½ cup chicken broth. Return to heat and cook for 2 minutes, stirring occasionally. Add the chicken, peppers, and tomatoes. Salt to taste and simmer, stirring occasionally, for 25 to 30 minutes until chicken is cooked through. In a small bowl, mix sour cream and flour. Place chicken on a platter. Stir sour cream mixture into vegetable mixture and add the remaining chicken broth. Simmer and stir for 3 minutes. Season the sauce with salt and pepper and spoon over the chicken. Serve with rice or noodles.

Yield: 4 servings.

CANARD L'ORANGE (ROAST DUCK WITH ORANGES)

4 whole seedless oranges
1 (4 to 5 pound) duckling
Salt and freshly ground pepper, to taste
¾ cup fresh or canned chicken broth
¼ cup sugar
¼ cup red wine vinegar
1 teaspoon cornstarch
1 tablespoon water
2 tablespoons Grand Marnier

Preheat oven to 375°. Using a vegetable peeler, peel and reserve the zest of 1 orange. (Rind only, no pulp). Cut the zest into very fine strips (julienne). Drop the strips into boiling water and simmer about 30 seconds. Drain and set aside. Completely peel all the oranges and carefully section them, cutting on either side of the membranes. There should be about 1½ cups of sections, set aside. Truss the duck with string and sprinkle it inside and out with salt and pepper. Chop the neck into 1 or 2-inch lengths. Cut away the tough outer membrane of the gizzard. Sprinkle the pieces of neck and gizzard with salt and pepper. Place the duck on its back in a roasting pan. Surround it with the neck pieces and gizzard. Place in the oven and bake for 30 minutes. Remove the pan and pour or spoon off the accumulated fat. Turn the duck on its side and return to the oven. Bake for 30 minutes. Remove the pan and spoon or pour off the fat. Take care not to pour off the juices in the pan. Increase oven temperature to 400°. Turn the duck breast side down and return to the oven. Bake for 30 minutes. Turn the duck on its other side and bake for 30 minutes. Remove the pan. Remove and discard the string from the duck. Transfer the duck, backside down, to another roasting pan. Return to the oven for 10 more minutes. Meanwhile, place the original roasting pan on top of the stove and add the chicken broth, stirring and scraping with a wooden spoon to dissolve the brown particles that cling to the bottom and side of the pan. Bring to a boil. Strain into a pan. Blend the sugar and vinegar in a very small saucepan and cook, watching carefully, until large bubbles form on the surface. Continue cooking until the syrup is thickened and slightly caramelized. Add the sauce from the roasting pan. Bring to a boil. Blend the cornstarch and water and stir into the sauce. Just before serving, add the zest and the Grand Marnier to the sauce. Drain the orange sections and add them. Cook, stirring gently, just until sections are thoroughly heated. Do not break them in stirring and do not overcook or they will become mushy. Serve the duck cut into quarters or carved. Pour a little of the sauce over the duck and serve the remainder separately.

Yield: 4 servings.

GLAZED CORNISH HENS WITH CURRIED RICE

3 (6 ounce) packages curried rice mix
¼ cup chopped drained chutney
12 (1 pound each) frozen Rock Cornish hens, thawed
½ cup butter or margarine, melted
1 (12 ounce) jar apricot preserves
¼ cup lemon juice

STUFFING

½ cup butter or margarine
1 cup chopped onion
2½ quarts fresh white breadcrumbs (10 cups)
2 cloves garlic, crushed
¼ cup chopped celery
⅓ cup dry white wine
½ teaspoon dried rosemary leaves
1 cup slivered blanched almonds
2 teaspoons salt
⅛ teaspoon pepper

Prepare rice as package label directs. Drain, if necessary. Stir in chutney. Refrigerate the rice mixture, covered, for several hours or until well chilled. Preheat oven to 450°. Make stuffing by sautéing onion in butter or margarine until tender, about 5 minutes. In a large bowl, lightly toss the sautéed onion with remaining ingredients. Wash Cornish hens well. Drain and pat dry with paper towels. Fill each with some of the stuffing. Close cavities of each with skewers; tie legs together with twine. Arrange hens in 2 large roasting pans. Brush with some of melted butter. Roast the hens, uncovered, 40 minutes. Brush each with melted butter every 10 minutes. Meanwhile, in small saucepan, melt preserves over low heat. Stir in lemon juice. Brush hens with preserve mixture. Roast hens for 20 to 25 minutes longer, or until nicely glazed and hens are tender. Legs should move easily. To serve, arrange hens on a bed of cold curried rice.

Yield: 12 servings.

MOULES MARINIERE (MUSSELS IN WHITE WINE)

2½ pounds cleaned mussels (approximately 2 quarts)
2 tablespoons butter
2 tablespoons finely chopped onion
1 tablespoon finely chopped green onions
1 small clove garlic, finely minced
2 tablespoons finely chopped parsley, divided
Freshly ground pepper
¾ cup dry white wine

Run the mussels under cold running water, rubbing the shells together to clean well. Drain. Heat the butter in a large pot and add the onion, green onion, and garlic. Cook until wilted and add the mussels. Add half the parsley, pepper to taste, and the wine. Cover tightly and cook for about 5 minutes, or until the mussels open. Serve mussels and broth in soup bowls sprinkled with remaining parsley. Serve with plenty of French bread.

Hint: Do not cook any mussels that are already open. Do not eat any mussels that do not open.

Yield: 2 to 4 servings.

ALISON'S SALMON

FISH

3 pounds fillet of salmon (skin on)
Olive oil
4 small boiling onions or 1 medium white onion
1 cup white wine
1-1½ cups water (depending on size of poaching pan)
Coarse ground black pepper
1 bunch fresh dill
½ lemon

SAUCE

1 pint Kefir (or crème fraîche)
1 bunch fresh dill
1 medium clove garlic
½ lemon
Coarse ground pepper
Salt

Rinse salmon under cold water and dry with a paper towel. Slice onions into small rings. Sauté in oil until translucent. Remove and set aside. Place salmon in poacher, skin side down. Pour the wine and water over the fish. Water should be at least 1-inch deep. Pepper fish lightly all over, scatter onions and olive oil over fish, top with ½ of the dill. Cover poacher and position over two burners. Both burners should be set at just below medium. The fat end of the fish should be over a slightly higher burner than the skinny end. Poach for no more than 20 minutes. You want the center of the salmon to remain moist. Remove poacher from stove and plunge into sink filled with cold tap water. Open poacher and carefully lift basket that supports fish out. Invert fish onto a platter skin side up. Remove skin and the layer of fatty gray flesh with a spatula. Pour about ¼ cup poaching liquid over fish. Chop remainder of the first bunch of dill over the fish and garnish with lemon rings. Allow fish to cool at least 1 hour before serving. Make sauce by taking the second bunch of dill, removing stems and mincing with the garlic. This can be done in a food processor. Add the juice of ½ lemon. Mix with Kefir or crème fraîche. Salt and pepper to taste. Let stand at least 1 hour before serving.

Hint: Kefir is available in health food stores.

Yield: 8 servings.

SALMON SOUFFLÉ

3 tablespoons butter or margarine
3 tablespoons all-purpose flour
1 teaspoon salt
½ teaspoon dry mustard
½ teaspoon Worcestershire sauce
1 (16 ounce) can salmon
1 cup milk
4 eggs, separated

About 1 hour and 15 minutes before serving, preheat oven to 375°. Grease a 1½ quart soufflé dish or casserole. In medium saucepan over medium heat, melt butter or margarine. Stir in flour, salt, mustard and Worcestershire until blended. Slowly stir in milk and cook, stirring constantly, until thickened. Cool about 10 minutes. Beat in egg yolks one at a time. In medium bowl, flake undrained salmon and stir into mixture. In large bowl, with electric mixer at high speed, beat egg whites until stiff peaks form. Fold gently into salmon mixture. Lightly pour into dish and bake 40 to 45 minutes until puffy and golden. Serve immediately.

Yield: 4 servings.

TRUITES A' L'ARDENNAISE

4 trout fillets
Salt and pepper
Flour
Butter
4 slices prosciutto, chopped
¼ cup browned breadcrumbs
Chopped parsley
Lemon

Lightly salt and pepper trout then coat with flour and brown them in hot butter on both sides. Keep warm. Mix prosciutto with breadcrumbs and warm slightly in frying pan, divide over fish. Decorate with parsley and sprinkle with lemon juice.

Yield: 4 servings.

SALMON WITH CUCUMBER SAUCE

Fish

2 pounds fresh salmon fillet
½ cup each finely chopped onion, carrots, celery and parsley (microwaved for 2 minutes)
Salt and pepper to taste
Lemon slices

Sauce

2-3 cucumbers peeled, seeded, and chopped
1 small onion
¼ cup vinegar
1½ cups sour cream

Combine onion, carrots, celery, and parsley and place in bottom of baking dish sized to accommodate fish. Season fish and place skin side down on mixture. Cover fish with thinly sliced lemon. Cover dish with foil and bake for 20 minutes in 350° oven, or until fish flakes. Remove skin and fat and place on platter. Spoon vegetables around fish. Garnish with fresh parsley and lemon. To make cucumber sauce, combine cucumber and very thinly sliced onion. Soak in ice water and vinegar, to cover, for awhile until very crisp. Drain well and add sour cream. Season to taste.

Hint: Can be served hot or cold.

Yield: 4 to 6 servings.

PEPPERY GARLIC SHRIMP WITH SHERRY SAUCE

1 cup dry sherry
10 tablespoons olive oil, divided
4 tablespoons fresh lemon juice
12 garlic cloves, minced
¼-½ teaspoon cayenne pepper
6 tablespoons chopped fresh parsley
1½ pounds large uncooked shrimp, peeled and deveined

Boil sherry, 2 tablespoons oil, lemon juice, garlic and cayenne pepper in a small, heavy saucepan until reduced to ½ cup, about 7 minutes. Transfer mixture to blender. With machine running, gradually add 6 tablespoons oil and blend until smooth sauce forms. Season to taste with salt and pepper. Add parsley and blend using on/off turns. Heat remaining 2 tablespoons oil in a medium, heavy skillet over high heat. Add shrimp and sauté until just cooked through, about 5 minutes. Divide shrimp between plates. Pour sauce over.

Yield: 4 servings.

SHRIMP ANNIE

- ¼ cup butter
- 1 small onion, finely chopped
- 1 pound raw gulf shrimp, peeled and deveined
- 1 (6 ounce) can mushrooms, drained
- 1 tablespoon flour
- Dash cayenne pepper
- ¼ teaspoon salt
- 1 cup sour cream
- 1½ cups cooked rice

Sauté onion in butter for 10 minutes or until tender. Add shrimp and mushrooms and sauté for 5 minutes more. Sprinkle in flour, salt and pepper. Stir in sour cream and cook gently for 10 minutes. Do not allow mixture to boil. Serve over rice.

Yield: 4 servings.

GAMBAS AL AJILLO

- ½ cup olive oil
- 8 large cloves garlic, finely minced
- 2 teaspoons red pepper flakes
- 2 pounds shrimp, peeled and deveined
- 4 tablespoons fresh lemon juice
- 4 tablespoons tequila or dry sherry
- 2 teaspoons paprika
- Salt and pepper
- Chopped Italian parsley

Warm olive oil in a large sauté pan over medium heat. Add garlic and red pepper flakes and sauté for 1 minute. Raise heat to high and add shrimp, lemon juice, tequila or sherry, and paprika. Stir well and sauté until the shrimp are done. Season to taste. Toss in chopped parsley.

Yield: 4 servings.

DAVID'S BBQ SHRIMP

½ pound margarine
¾ teaspoon basil
¾ teaspoon garlic salt
2 tablespoons coarse ground black pepper
3 pounds shrimp, shells on, heads removed
¼ cup olive oil
1 tablespoon parsley flakes
½ teaspoon oregano
¾ teaspoon salt
2 tablespoons lemon juice

Melt margarine in shallow pan and add remaining ingredients, except shrimp, and stir well. Place shrimp in a broiler pan and coat well with sauce. Bake in a 450° oven for 10 minutes. Stir often to distribute sauce. Broil for 5 minutes.

Yield: 6 to 8 servings.

DESSERT COLLECTION

Charles-Joseph Natoire, French, 1700-1777
Bacchanal, c. 1747
Oil on canvas, 31⅞ x 39⅞ in.
The Museum of Fine Arts, Houston, museum purchase

In a classical scene of abandoned merrymaking Bacchus, the ancient god of the vine, exuberantly enjoys a feast while being tended by his Bacchantes. In the Rococo style the composition is animated by flowing lines, billowing clothes, swaying trees and curving bodies. The luxurious and vibrant colors and often transparent pigments contribute to the mood and atmospheric quality. Such sensuous and decorative pieces were much favored by French tastes and in the court of Louis XV in the mid-eighteenth century.

Dessert Collection

Apricot Whip
Rhoda's Pound Cake
Apricot Brandy Pound Cake
Pumpkin Cake
Dump Coffee Cake
Black Russian Cake
The Best Cake (Really)
Buttermilk Glaze Icing
Passover Sponge Cake
Grandma Moses' Gingerbread
The Best Chocolate Cake
Chocolate Chip Cake
Vanilla Wafer Cake
Lady Finger Mousse Cake
Chocolate Delight
Masterson Family Frozen Fruitcake
Boiled Custard
Rose Bowles' Fabulous Fruitcake
Seven Up Cake
Mary Anne Varner's Little Lizzies
Cake Roll
Mousse au Chocolat
Lemon Chess Pie
Tony's Delicious Cheesecake
Cinnamon Pecans
Iced Chocolate and Brandy Creams
Microwave Pecan Brittle
Pralines (from Brennan's)
Microwave Chocolate Peanut Clusters
Chocolate Mint Bars
Chocolate Mint Mousse
Mocha Pie
Fudge Pie
Brandy Alexander Pie
Lime Pie
Chocolate Delight Pie
Dream Pie
German Chocolate Angel Pie
Patrician Peach Pie
Helen Corbitt's Grasshopper Pie
Rich Kentucky Oatmeal Pie
Margarita Pie
Pecan Pie
Grandma's Apple Crisp
Saratoga Torte
Apple Bavarian Torte
Date Balls
Quick Chewy Bar Cookies
Tweety's Famous Cookies
Apricot Jumbles
Pumpkin-Chocolate Chip Cookies
No Bake Chocolate Oatmeal Drop Cookies
Dried Cranberry and White Chocolate Biscotti
Lemon Squares
Lemon Curd
White Chocolate-Macadamia Chunk Cookies
Brittle Cracker Cookies
Aunt Linda Ade's Ginger Cookies
Absolutely Wonderful Sand Tarts
Snowflake Spritz Cookies
Brownies
Crème De Menthe Brownies
Club Cracker Crunch
Texas Brownies
Rienzi's Brownies with Fudge Icing
Caramel Chocolate Squares
Frozen Lemon Mousse
Pumpkin Ice Cream Pie
Peach Marlow
Pears in Red Wine
Sweet Kugel
White Wine Granita with Blackberries
Sherried Fruit Compote
Chocolate Meringues
Oregon Blackberry Meringue Cups
Aunt Edith's Chocolate Sauce
Meringue Forgetums
Chewy Pecan Pie Squares
Sweet Wonton "Napoleon"
Swedish Nut Balls
Frozen Cherry Cream
Fudge Sauce for Ice Cream
"Ravo"
Orange Soufflé

APRICOT WHIP

½ teaspoon canola, corn or safflower oil
6 tablespoons sugar, divided
5 ounces dried California apricots
½ cup coarsely chopped walnuts, toasted
1 teaspoon vanilla extract
5 egg whites, room temperature

Brush a 6 to 8 cup gratin dish with the oil and coat the bottom and sides of the dish with 2 tablespoons of the sugar (shake the dish to distribute the sugar evenly). Set aside. Place the apricots in a medium saucepan and add enough water to cover them. Bring the water to a boil, reduce the heat to low and cook the apricots at a gentle boil for about 10 minutes, until they are tender when pierced with the point of a sharp knife. Drain the apricots and chop them coarsely. (There should be about 1 generous cup of apricot pieces.) In a small bowl, mix together the apricots, walnuts and vanilla. Set aside. Preheat the oven to 375°. Place the egg whites in a large copper or stainless steel mixing bowl. Beat by hand with a large balloon whisk or with an electric mixer (fitted with a whisk attachment) at medium to high speed. When the whites hold a firm peak, gradually add the remaining 4 tablespoons sugar, then keep beating the mixture for 10 seconds. The whites should be stiff and shiny. Gently fold the reserved apricot mixture into the egg whites. Pour the mixture into the prepared dish and bake for 20 to 25 minutes, until the dessert is puffy and lightly browned on top. Cool and serve lukewarm or at room temperature with biscotti or cookies.

Yield: 6 servings.

RHODA'S POUND CAKE

3 cups granulated sugar
1½ cups butter
6 eggs
1 cup sour cream
3 cups sifted all-purpose flour
¼ teaspoon baking soda
1 teaspoon vanilla extract

Cream sugar and softened butter until light and fluffy. Add one egg at a time to the mixture. Gradually add sour cream and dry ingredients, beating until the batter is smooth. Stir in vanilla. Bake in a greased and floured tube pan at 350° for 1 hour and 15 minutes. Let stand in pan for 10 minutes. Place on cake rack to cool.

Yield: 12 servings.

APRICOT BRANDY POUND CAKE

3 cups sugar
1 cup unsalted margarine
6 eggs
3 cups flour
¼ teaspoon baking soda
½ teaspoon salt
1 cup sour cream
1 teaspoon orange extract
¼ teaspoon almond extract
½ teaspoon lemon extract
1 teaspoon vanilla extract
½ cup apricot brandy

Cream butter and sugar. Add eggs, one at a time. Add other ingredients in order listed; alternately add flour and sour cream (after all other ingredients are combined). Be sure to add flour and sour cream in small quantities until well blended. Bake in greased and floured tube pan for about 1 hour and 10 minutes at 325°.

Yield: 10 servings.

PUMPKIN CAKE

3 cups sugar
1 cup butter
3 eggs
1 (15 to 16 ounce) can pumpkin
1 teaspoon vanilla
3 cups flour
1 teaspoon soda
¼ teaspoon salt
½ teaspoon baking powder
1 teaspoon cloves
1 teaspoon nutmeg
1 teaspoon cinnamon
1 teaspoon allspice

Preheat oven to 350°. Grease and flour tube or Bundt pan. Cream sugar with butter. Lightly beat eggs and add to sugar and shortening. Add pumpkin, Add vanilla. Sift flour with dry ingredients. Add to egg mixture until well blended. Pour into prepared pan. Bake 1 hour. Let cool 20 minutes and invert onto plate. Dust with powdered sugar or favorite glaze.

Yield: 10 servings.

DUMP COFFEE CAKE

2 eggs, slightly beaten
2 cups sugar
½ cup cooking oil
2 cups flour
1 (21 ounce) can prepared apple pie filling
1 teaspoon baking soda
2 cups chopped pecans
1 teaspoon salt
1 teaspoon vanilla
1 teaspoon cinnamon

"Dump" all ingredients into a bowl and mix together. Bake in a greased and floured 13 X 9 X 2 inch pan at 350° for one hour.

Yield: 24 servings.

BLACK RUSSIAN CAKE

Cake

1 yellow cake mix
½ cup sugar
1 (8 ounce) package chocolate instant pudding
1 cup vegetable oil
4 eggs
¼ cup vodka
¼ cup Kahlúa
¾ cup water

Glaze

½ cup powdered sugar
¼ cup Kahlúa

Mix all ingredients well and beat 4 minutes. Pour into Bundt pan sprayed with non-stick cooking spray. Bake at 350° for 45 to 50 minutes. Cool in pan for 10 minutes, then remove from pan. As cake cools in pan prepare glaze. To prepare glaze, mix powdered sugar and Kahlúa together until there are no lumps. Spoon onto hot cake.

Yield: 8 servings.

THE BEST CAKE (REALLY)

2 cups sugar
2 cups flour
1 teaspoon cinnamon
1 teaspoon salt
1 teaspoon baking soda
½ teaspoon nutmeg
3 eggs
1 cup mashed prunes
1 cup buttermilk
1 cup chopped pecans
⅔ cup vegetable oil
Glaze, optional (recipe follows)

Combine all ingredients and mix well. Pour into greased Bundt pan. Bake at 325° for 1 hour.

Hint: If using dried, pitted prunes, place 1½ cups prunes in pan with 1½ cups water. Bring to a boil, reduce heat, and simmer 10 minutes covered. Drain and mash to get 1 cup prunes.

Yield: 8 to 10 servings.

BUTTERMILK GLAZE ICING

½ cup sugar
¼ cup buttermilk
¼ cup butter

Combine and stir well. Cook 6 to 7 minutes at low boil over low heat. Pour over cooled cake.

PASSOVER SPONGE CAKE

8 eggs
1½ cups sugar
1 tablespoon fresh lemon juice
Grated rind of one lemon
2 tablespoons fresh orange juice
Grated rind of one orange
¾ cup sifted potato starch

Separate 6 eggs and add 2 whole eggs to the yolk mixture. Using an electric mixer, beat yolk mixture until thick and lemon-colored. Continue beating and add sugar, lemon juice and rind, and orange juice and rind. Gradually beat in potato starch. Set aside. Beat separated egg whites until stiff. Fold egg whites very slowly and gently into potato starch mixture by hand. Do not beat. This is the most important step. Combine gently but thoroughly. Pour into ungreased, 2 piece, 10 inch tubular pan. Bake in 325° oven for about 1 hour and 10 minutes. Do not open oven for first hour. Be sure cake tests dry with toothpick before removing from oven. Invert cake and allow to cool thoroughly before removing from pan.

Yield: 10 servings.

GRANDMA MOSES' GINGERBREAD

1 cup sugar
2 tablespoons molasses
2 tablespoons butter
2 tablespoons lard or shortening
1 teaspoon baking soda
½ teaspoon ginger
½ teaspoon cloves
Pinch of salt
2 cups flour
1 egg
1 cup buttermilk

Beat all ingredients together and bake for 45 minutes in a buttered 9 inch square pan at 350°.

Yield: 8 to 12 servings.

THE BEST CHOCOLATE CAKE

Cake

2 cups flour
2 cups sugar
½ teaspoon salt
1 cup butter
1 cup water
3 heaping tablespoons cocoa
2 eggs, beaten
1 teaspoon vanilla
1 teaspoon soda
½ cup buttermilk

Icing

½ cup butter
3 heaping teaspoons cocoa
1 (1 pound) box powdered sugar
1 teaspoon vanilla
Milk
1 cup chopped walnuts

To prepare cake, combine flour, sugar, and salt in a mixing bowl. Bring butter, water, and cocoa to a boil in a saucepan. Add to dry mixture. Add eggs, vanilla, soda and buttermilk. Beat well with a whisk until mixed. Bake in a 13 X 9 X 2 inch, greased, and floured pan for 20 to 25 minutes at 350°. If using dark pan, bake at 325°. Ice as soon as you remove from oven. To make icing, melt butter in saucepan then add cocoa, stirring until well mixed. Add powdered sugar, vanilla, and enough milk to make a spread. Add nuts. Spread on warm cake.

Hint: To make buttermilk, put 2 tablespoons lemon juice and enough milk to equal ½ cup. Let sit for 10 minutes.

CHOCOLATE CHIP CAKE

1 chocolate cake mix (German or fudge)
1 large box (or 2 small boxes) instant chocolate pudding
1 cup vegetable oil
¼ cup milk
4 eggs
1 (8 ounce) container sour cream
1 tablespoon vanilla
1 cup chopped pecans
1 (12 ounce) package chocolate chips (milk chocolate or semi-sweet)

Mix first 7 ingredients together. Beat 3 minutes. Add pecans and chocolate chips, beating on low only until well incorporated. Bake at 350° for 50 to 60 minutes or until toothpick comes out clean. Cool in pan 10 minutes, then remove from pan.

Yield: 16 servings.

VANILLA WAFER CAKE

1 (12 ounce) box vanilla wafers, crushed finely
1 cup butter
2 cups sugar
6 eggs
½ cup milk
1 (13 to 14 ounce) can coconut
1 cup chopped pecans

Crush vanilla wafers until very fine. Set aside. Cream butter thoroughly. Gradually add sugar until very well blended. Add eggs one at a time, beating well after each addition. Add vanilla wafer crumbs alternately with milk, beginning and ending with crumbs. Add coconut and pecans, beating on low speed only until well incorporated. Pour into a greased and floured tube or Bundt pan. Bake at 350° for 1 hour and 15 minutes (start checking after 1 hour) until toothpick comes out clean. Cool in pan for 10 minutes, then remove.

Yield: 12 servings.

LADY FINGER MOUSSE CAKE

1 (12 ounce) package chocolate chips
4½ teaspoons water
6 eggs, separated
2 teaspoons vanilla
2 tablespoons sugar
2 cups heavy cream
36 lady fingers, unfilled

Melt chocolate with 4½ teaspoons water. Cool. Beat in one egg yolk at a time, add vanilla. Beat egg whites until stiff and gradually beat in sugar until stiff peaks form. Beat half of white mixture into chocolate. Fold in remaining egg whites. Make whip cream by beating at high speed and add 1 tablespoon sugar. Fold in ¾ of whip cream into chocolate. Line sides, then bottom, of a 9 inch springform pan with lady fingers, uncut side facing out. Pour in ⅓ of chocolate. Layer more lady fingers. Alternating layers and ending with chocolate on top. Garnish with remaining whipped cream. Refrigerate 1 hour before serving.

Yield: 12 servings.

CHOCOLATE DELIGHT

1 (12 ounce) package German sweet chocolate
1 tablespoon water
2 eggs, separated
1 teaspoon vanilla
½ pint whip cream (whipped)
1 teaspoon confectioners' sugar
1 package lady fingers

Melt chocolate with water in a double boiler. Cool somewhat and add 2 beaten egg yolks, then 2 beaten egg whites. Add vanilla and set aside. Add the sugar to the whipped cream. In a serving bowl, layer the ingredients as follows: Chocolate mixture, lady fingers, chocolate mixture, whipped cream, lady fingers, chocolate mixture and top with whipped cream.

Yield: 6 to 8 servings.

MASTERSON FAMILY FROZEN FRUITCAKE

1 pint cream, whipped
1 pint boiled custard (recipe follows)
1 cup white raisins
1 cup lady fingers, crumbled
1 cup almond macaroons, crumbled
1 cup pecans, chopped coarsely

Whip cream. Add cookies, raisins, and nuts to custard. Then fold custard mixture into whipped cream. Pour in a lightly buttered 10 cup mold and freeze.

Yield: 12 servings.

BOILED CUSTARD

2 cups milk
4 egg yolks, beaten
¼ cup sugar
⅛ teaspoon salt
1 teaspoon vanilla

Scald 2 cups milk in top of double boiler. Remove from heat and stir in a small amount of the hot milk into egg yolks that have been beaten. Return mixture to top of double boiler and add ¼ cup sugar and ⅛ teaspoon salt. Stir constantly over medium heat until custard thickens. (Custard thickens a little after cooling.) Remove from heat and add 1 teaspoon vanilla. Beat with spoon to release heat from custard. Cool in refrigerator before adding to fruitcake.

Hint: The frozen fruitcake was inverted onto a platter with a small rim. Eggnog was placed in a footed bowl in the center of the fruitcake. A small ladle of very thick homemade eggnog was spooned over each serving of cake.

ROSE BOWLES' FABULOUS FRUITCAKE

1 pound candied cherries
1 pound pitted dates
1 pound candied pineapple chunks
1 pound pecans
1½ cups flour, divided
4 eggs
1 cup sugar
½ teaspoon salt
1 teaspoon baking powder
1 tablespoon vanilla extract

In a large mixing bowl, combine fruits and nuts with ½ cup flour. In a medium size mixing bowl, beat eggs until fluffy. Add sugar, remaining cup of flour, salt, baking powder, and vanilla. Beat until mixed. Add egg mixture to fruit and nuts. Mixing by hands is the best way to mix it. Bake in a greased and floured Bundt pan for 1 hour and 30 minutes at 325°.

Hint: It is not necessary to chop fruit and nuts prior to baking.

Yield: 20 servings.

SEVEN-UP CAKE

1½ cups butter
3 cups sugar
5 jumbo eggs
3 cups flour
2 tablespoons lemon extract
¾ cup lemon-lime flavored carbonated beverage (not Sprite)
¼ cup powdered sugar

Cream together butter and sugar for about 25 minutes or until light and fluffy Add eggs, one at a time, and cream well after each. Add flour, lemon extract and carbonated beverage. Bake in greased and floured pan (tube or Bundt) for 1 hour and 15 minutes at 325°. Remove from pan and when cool, dust with powdered sugar.

Yield: 8 to 10 servings.

MARY ANNE VARNER'S LITTLE LIZZIES

¼ cup margarine or butter
½ cup light brown sugar
2 eggs
1½ cups flour
1½ teaspoons baking soda
½ teaspoon cloves
½ teaspoon nutmeg
1½ teaspoons cinnamon
1 pound white raisins
½ cup bourbon
1 pound pecans, chopped
1 pound candied cherries, chopped
½ pound citron
½ pound pineapple

Soak the raisins in the bourbon overnight. Cream the margarine or butter with the sugar. Add the eggs and beat well. Sift together the flour, baking soda, and spices. Add the raisins, nuts and fruits. Mix together. Combine all the mixtures together in a large bowl. Drop by spoonfuls onto greased cookie sheets. Bake at 325° for 15 minutes.

Yield: 10 dozen.

CAKE ROLL

4 eggs, separated
¾ cup sugar, divided
½ teaspoon vanilla
¾ cup sifted flour
¼ teaspoon salt
1 teaspoon baking powder
½ cup confectioners' sugar
2 pints vanilla ice cream
1 quart strawberries

Separate eggs. Beat egg yolks until lemon colored and thick. Gradually add ¼ cup sugar and vanilla. Beat the egg whites until almost stiff. Gradually add ½ cup sugar and beat until very stiff. Fold yolk mixture into whites. Combine flour, salt, and baking powder. Fold into egg mixture. Turn into a 15 X 10 inch sheet pan that has been greased and lined with waxed paper. Bake in a 375° oven for 12 minutes. Loosen edges of cake. Turn out on towel that has been spread with confectioners' sugar. Pull wax paper off as quickly as possible. Cut off hard edges. Put sheet of waxed paper over cake and roll (jelly roll style). Wrap in towel with confectioners' sugar. Let cool. Unroll and spread with ice cream. Roll up again, wrap in waxed paper and foil and freeze several hours. Slice in appropriately thick slices and serve with sliced strawberries.

Variation: Use different flavored ice cream and toppings. One example is Pralines and Cream ice cream topped with toasted almonds.

Yield: 8 to 10 servings.

MOUSSE AU CHOCOLAT

¾ cup semi-sweet chocolate chips
2 tablespoons unsalted butter
4 eggs, separated
2 tablespoons Kahlúa (or very strong coffee)
⅓ cup sugar
Sweetened whipped cream, optional

Melt chocolate chips and butter together in a large bowl in a very slow oven. Add Kahlúa and egg yolks. Mix. In a separate bowl, beat egg whites until soft peaks form. Add sugar a little at a time and whip until firm. Using a rubber spatula, fold egg whites into chocolate mixture. Pour into serving dish or individual bowls and refrigerate for a minimum of 6 hours. Serve very cold. May be frozen.

Yield: 6 servings.

LEMON CHESS PIE

1½ cups sugar
4 teaspoons cornstarch
2 teaspoons finely grated lemon peel
4 eggs, room temperature
⅓ cup fresh lemon juice
5 tablespoons unsalted butter, melted and cooled
1 partially baked pie shell

Preheat oven to 325°. Combine sugar and cornstarch in bowl and mix, pressing out lumps. Stir in lemon peel. Beat in eggs, one at a time. Stir in lemon juice. Add butter. Pour in pie shell. Bake until puffed and golden, 50 to 60 minutes. Cool to room temperature before serving.

Yield: 6 to 8 servings.

TONY'S DELICIOUS CHEESECAKE

1 pound creamed cottage cheese
1 pound cream cheese, softened
1½ cups sugar
4 eggs
1 teaspoon vanilla
3 tablespoons cornstarch
3 tablespoons flour
¼ pound butter, melted
16 ounces sour cream

Cream cottage and cream cheeses together until well creamed. Add sugar. Add eggs one at a time and beat well after each addition. Stir in vanilla, cornstarch and flour. Add melted butter and blend well. Add sour cream. Pour into well greased 10 inch springform pan. Bake in a 325° oven until firm, approximately 1 hour and 15 minutes. Turn oven off and leave cake in oven while cooling for about 2 hours. Do not cut for several hours.

Hint: Can be made the day before and refrigerated after cooling.

Yield: 14 to 16 servings.

CINNAMON PECANS

1 egg white
1 teaspoon cold water
1 pound pecans
1 cup sugar
1¼ teaspoons ground cinnamon
Pinch of nutmeg
1 teaspoon salt

Preheat oven to 225°. Grease a baking sheet. In a bowl, combine sugar, cinnamon, nutmeg and salt. Set aside. In a large mixing bowl, beat egg white and water with a whisk until frothy. Add pecans to egg white and stir to coat pecans. Add sugar mixture to pecans and stir to coat pecans. Spread on greased cookie sheet. Bake at 225° for 50 minutes, stirring occasionally.

Yield: 4 cups.

ICED CHOCOLATE AND BRANDY CREAMS

- **½ pint double cream (available at specialty markets)**
- **6 ounces dark chocolate**
- **3 large egg yolks**
- **3 tablespoons honey, heated until very hot**
- **3 tablespoons brandy**

Put the cream in a saucepan and break the chocolate into it. Over a gentle heat, melt the chocolate in the cream, stirring until both cream and chocolate are well combined. Take the saucepan off the heat and cool the cream mixture. It will thicken as it cools, so take care not to let it become too stiff to fold into the yolk mixture. Put the egg yolks into a bowl and pour on the hot honey, beat vigorously with an electric mixer. Continue beating until the yolks become very pale and thick, then beat in the brandy. Fold together the chocolate cream and the yolk and honey mixtures, and divide among the ramekins. Freeze the ramekins on a tray, uncovered, then when they are quite hard, cover each ramekin and freeze.

Yield: 8 servings.

MICROWAVE PECAN BRITTLE

- **1 cup chopped pecans**
- **1 cup white sugar**
- **½ cup light corn syrup**
- **1 teaspoon butter**
- **1 teaspoon vanilla**
- **1 teaspoon baking soda**

Combine sugar and corn syrup in a 1½ quart microwave safe bowl. Stir well. Microwave on high for 4 minutes. Stir in pecans and microwave on high for 5 to 7 minutes or until lightly browned. Stir in butter and vanilla. Microwave on medium for 1 minute. Stir in baking soda until foamy. Pour mixture onto a previously lightly greased baking sheet. Cool baking sheet on a wire rack. Break into pieces and store in an airtight container.

Yield: ¾ pound.

PRALINES (FROM BRENNAN'S)

1 cup heavy cream
3 cups sugar
1½ pounds chopped pecans (6 cups)
Juice of 1 lemon

In a heavy saucepan, slowly simmer cream and sugar over low heat until the mixture becomes golden brown in color and reaches the soft-ball stage. Add pecans and lemon juice and continue to cook until the soft-ball stage is reached again. Drop from a large kitchen spoon onto an oiled baking sheet or a marble slab moistened with water. Spread each praline out with back of spoon to about ¼ inch thick and 4 to 5 inches in diameter. Let harden, (it helps to let harden in sunlight or strong light) then lift from pan or slab with a spatula. Pralines will keep for 2 weeks in a covered tin at room temperature.

Hint: Soft-ball stage is reached when a small amount of syrup dropped into ice water holds its shape without separating into threads.

Yield: 2 dozen.

MICROWAVE CHOCOLATE PEANUT CLUSTERS

1 package chocolate bark
1 (8 ounce) can dry roasted peanuts

Put 6 to 12 squares of chocolate bark into a 2 quart microwave safe bowl. Microwave on high for 1 minute 50 seconds to 2 minutes. Stir halfway through. When melted and easy to stir, remove and add peanuts. Stir until peanuts are covered. Drop onto waxed paper by tablespoon.

Yield: 2 to 3 dozen.

CHOCOLATE MINT BARS

4 eggs
1 cup white sugar
1 cup flour
16 ounces chocolate syrup
3 cups margarine, divided
3 cups powdered sugar
1 teaspoon mint extract
1½ cups semi-sweet chocolate chips
3 squares of baker's chocolate

Preheat oven to 350°. In a bowl, mix eggs, sugar, flour, chocolate syrup, and ½ cup margarine. Pour the mixture into a greased 13 X 9 X 2 inch jelly-roll pan and bake for 25 to 30 minutes. Cool. For the first topping, melt 1½ cups margarine and mix with powdered sugar and mint extract. Spread over first layer and cool. For the second topping, melt chocolate chips, baker's chocolate, and 1 cup margarine and mix together. Spread over second layer and cool.

Yield: 12 servings.

CHOCOLATE MINT MOUSSE

20 chocolate covered mints
1 cup semi-sweet chocolate morsels
⅓ cup sugar
3 eggs
1 cup milk
½ pint whipping cream

Place mints, chocolate morsels, sugar and eggs in blender. Blend for about 30 seconds. Scald milk. Add milk to mixture and mix until smooth. Pour into bowl and chill for 30 to 45 minutes or until mixture begins to set. Whip the cream and fold into chocolate mint mixture. Spoon into dessert dishes, if desired, and chill. May be garnished with whipped cream, grated chocolate, and fresh mint sprigs.

Yield: 6 to 8 servings.

MOCHA PIE

1 (11.95 ounce) jar hot fudge sauce, divided
1 (16 ounce) chocolate flavored crumb crust
1 pint coffee ice cream, softened
1 (2.07 ounce) chocolate coated caramel peanut nougat bars, chopped and divided
1 pint chocolate ice cream, softened
¼ cup slivered almonds, toasted

Spread half of fudge sauce onto crumb crust. Carefully spread coffee ice cream over sauce. Top with half the candy bar pieces. Cover and freeze at least 2 hours. Spread chocolate ice cream carefully over candy piece layer. Then spread remaining fudge sauce. Top with remaining half of candy and sprinkle with almonds. Cover and freeze until firm.

Yield: 8 servings.

FUDGE PIE

2 cups sugar
3 (1 ounce) squares bittersweet chocolate, melted
⅓ cup butter
⅛ teaspoon salt
1 cup chopped pecans
4 eggs
1 teaspoon vanilla
1 (9 inch) pie shell, unbaked

Preheat oven to 350°. Add melted chocolate, butter, salt and chopped nuts to sugar. Stir in eggs and vanilla. Pour into unbaked pie shell and bake for 40 minutes. Remove from oven before completely firm. Check with toothpick to make sure it is not runny. It is OK if top "cracks."

Yield: 8 servings.

BRANDY ALEXANDER PIE

1 envelope unflavored gelatin
½ cup cold water
⅔ cup sugar, divided
⅛ teaspoon salt
3 eggs, separated
¼ cup cognac
¼ cup crème de cacao
2 cups heavy cream, whipped, divided
Graham cracker crust
Chocolate curls

Sprinkle the gelatin over the cold water in saucepan. Add one third cup of the sugar, salt, and egg yolks. Stir to blend. Heat the gelatin mixture over low heat while stirring until the gelatin dissolves and the mixture thickens. Do not let it boil. Remove from heat and stir in cognac and crème de cacao. Freeze until the mixture starts to mound slightly. Beat the egg whites until stiff. Gradually beat in remaining sugar and fold into thickened gelatin mixture. Fold in one cup whipped cream. Freeze several hours or overnight. Garnish with remaining whipped cream and chocolate curls.

Note: This is a generous recipe. It will fill one large homemade graham cracker crust or 2 ready made crusts.

Yield: 6 to 8 servings .

LIME PIE

1 (14 ounce) can condensed milk, chilled
4 eggs, separated
½ cup lime juice
Graham cracker crust
Green food coloring, optional

Cook crust according to directions. Mix milk, lime juice and beaten egg yolks. Add food coloring, if desired. Fold in stiffly beaten egg whites and pour mixture into the crust. Bake at 350° for 10 to 20 minutes, or until top is lightly brown. Chill overnight before serving.

Yield: 10 servings.

CHOCOLATE DELIGHT PIE

1 (9 inch) baked pie shell
10 ounces (approximately) semi-sweet chocolate chips
3 eggs, separated
2 cups whipping cream, divided
1½ teaspoon vanilla, divided
¼ cup powdered sugar
Shaved chocolate, optional
Raspberries, optional

Melt chocolate chips in top of double boiler and then remove from heat. Beat 1 cup whipping cream until stiff. Beat 2 egg whites until stiff. Combine the 2 egg yolks, the remaining whole egg, and 1 teaspoon vanilla with the melted chocolate. Fold in the egg whites and whipped cream and put into the pie shell. Chill. Beat the remaining whipping cream, gradually adding the powdered sugar and remaining ½ teaspoon vanilla. Garnish pie with whipped cream. Top with shaved chocolate, raspberries, or garnish of your choice.

Yield: 8 servings.

DREAM PIE

3 tablespoons lemon juice
1 (14 ounce) can sweetened condensed milk
1 (8 ounce) can pineapple tidbits, drained
1 cup chopped pecans
1 (7 ounce) can coconut
1 (8 ounce) carton frozen non-dairy whipped topping
2 ready baked graham cracker pie crusts

Add lemon juice to milk, mix well. Add drained pineapple, nuts and coconut. Mix well. Fold in non-dairy whipped topping. Pour into pie crusts and chill.

Yield: 2 pies.

GERMAN CHOCOLATE ANGEL PIE

Crust

3 egg whites
⅛ teaspoon cream of tartar
¾ cup sugar
¾ cup chopped pecans

Filling

1 pint whipping cream
4 ounces German chocolate
3 tablespoons coffee, brewed

To prepare the crust, beat egg whites until frothy. Add cream of tartar. Beat until very stiff, adding ¼ cup sugar at a time. Beat in well. Add pecans. Spread in well buttered pie plate. Bake 50 minutes at 300°. To prepare filling, whip cream. Melt chocolate and add coffee. Fold in cream. Pour into cooled crust and refrigerate for 2 to 3 hours.

Yield: 6 to 8 servings.

PATRICIAN PEACH PIE

5 large, very ripe peaches
1 (9 inch) pie shell, unbaked
2 large eggs
1 cup granulated sugar
2 tablespoons all-purpose flour
1-2 teaspoons almond extract, according to taste

Preheat oven to 325°. Peel peaches by plunging into boiling water for approximately 10 seconds. Slice into pie shell. Beat eggs, sugar and flour together until smooth. Add almond extract. Pour over peaches. Bake 1 hour. Serve at room temperature.

Hint: Serve with vanilla ice cream and raspberries for garnish.

Variation: Ripe nectarines can be substituted for peaches and the pie will be just as splendid.

Yield: 6 to 8 servings.

HELEN CORBITT'S GRASSHOPPER PIE

20 plain chocolate wafers, crushed
⅓ cup melted butter
25 large marshmallows
½ cup milk
2 ounces crème de menthe
1 ounce white crème de cocoa
1½ cups whipping cream, divided
Shaved or grated semi-sweet chocolate

Mix the crushed cookies with butter and press into a lightly buttered 9 inch pie pan. Bake at 350° for 10 minutes. Cool. Melt the marshmallows in the milk in a double boiler. Cool, add the liqueurs and beat thoroughly. Whip the cream into soft peaks. Fold ⅔ of whipped cream into the cooled mixture. Pour all but ½ cup filling into the crust. Refrigerate until partially set. Pour remaining ½ cup filling into center of pie. Refrigerate for several hours or longer. Spread remaining whipped cream over top. Cover with shaved or grated chocolate.

Yield: 6 servings.

RICH KENTUCKY OATMEAL PIE

2 eggs, well beaten
⅔ cup sugar
1 teaspoon vanilla
⅔ cup corn syrup
¾ cup oatmeal
½ cup butter, melted
1 (9 inch) pie shell, unbaked

Mix all ingredients well and put into an unbaked 9 inch pie shell. Bake at 350° for 35 minutes or until center is done.

Yield: 8 servings.

MARGARITA PIE

½ cup + 2 tablespoons margarine
1¼ cups crushed pretzels
¼ cup sugar
⅓ cup sweetened condensed milk
⅓ cup lime juice
2 tablespoons tequila
2 tablespoons Triple Sec liqueur
8 ounces whipping cream, whipped
Green food coloring, optional
Lime slices, optional

To make crust, melt margarine and stir in pretzels and sugar. Mix well. Press into bottom and up sides of a 9 inch pie plate. Chill. Prepare filling by mixing condensed milk, lime juice, tequila, triple sec and food coloring, if desired. Blend well. Fold whipped cream into mixture. Top with lime slices, if desired. Freeze 4 hours before serving.

Yield: 8 servings.

PECAN PIE

4 eggs, beaten
1 cup light corn syrup
⅔ cup sugar
1 tablespoon butter, melted
1 teaspoon vanilla
1 cup coarsely chopped pecans
1 (9 inch) pie crust, unbaked

Combine eggs, syrup, sugar, butter, and vanilla. Beat with an electric mixer until blended. Stir in pecans. Pour mixture into unbaked pie crust and bake at 350° for 50 to 55 minutes.

Yield: 8 servings.

GRANDMA'S APPLE CRISP

1 cup flour
1 teaspoon baking powder
1 unbeaten egg
1½ cups sugar
¾ teaspoon salt
5-6 apples, tart red or green
¼ teaspoon cinnamon
⅓ cup melted butter

Lightly grease and flour a deep-dish 9 inch pie plate or coat with non-stick cooking spray. Set aside. In small bowl, combine flour, baking powder, egg, sugar and salt. Set aside. Core, peel and thinly slice apples. Arrange apples over the bottom of the pie plate. Sprinkle flour mixture over apples. Sprinkle with cinnamon. Pour melted butter over all ingredients and bake in a 350° oven for 25 minutes or until browned and crispy on top. Serve warm.

Yield: 6 to 8 servings.

SARATOGA TORTE

3 egg whites
1 cup sugar
14 small (2 X 2 inch) soda crackers, crumbled
¾ cup chopped walnuts or pecans
1 teaspoon baking powder
1 teaspoon vanilla
1 cup whipping cream, whipped
Grated unsweetened baking chocolate

Beat egg whites until partially stiff and then gradually add sugar. Combine crumbled crackers, nut and baking powder and fold into egg mixture along with vanilla. Spread into a 9 inch pie pan. Bake for 45 minutes at 350°. When cool, spread with whipped cream. Refrigerate at least 2 hours before serving. Grate unsweetened baking chocolate on top for garnish.

Yield: 8 servings.

APPLE BAVARIAN TORTE

Crust

- **½ cup butter, chilled**
- **⅓ cup granulated sugar**
- **1 cup sifted flour**
- **¼ teaspoon vanilla**

Filling

- **1 pound cream cheese**
- **½ cup sugar**
- **2 eggs, lightly beaten**
- **1 teaspoon vanilla**

Topping

- **3 medium cooking apples, peeled and sliced**
- **¼ cup sugar**
- **½ teaspoon cinnamon**
- **¼ teaspoon vanilla**
- **¼ cup coarsely chopped nuts**

To prepare crust, cut butter into very small pieces. Combine crust ingredients and mix together with pastry blender until mixture resembles coarse meal. Press into a 10 inch springform pan and bake for 5 minutes at 350°. To prepare filling, in large mixing bowl, combine cream cheese, sugar, eggs and vanilla. Mix until completely blended and pour into prepared crust. To prepare topping, mix sugar, cinnamon, and vanilla. Add to apple slices in a large bowl. Stir to mix well. Arrange apple slices on top of cheese mixture and sprinkle top with walnuts. Bake torte 15 minutes at 400°. Reduce heat to 350° and bake an additional 45 minutes. Cool to room temperature and chill.

Yield: 12 servings.

DATE BALLS

9 ounces dates, chopped
1 cup sugar
9 ounces butter
1 teaspoon vanilla
9 ounces (6 cups) crisp rice cereal
Pecans, chopped (optional)
Coconut

Combine dates, sugar, and butter into large, heavy saucepan. Stir continuously until all the butter has melted, the sugar dissolved and the mixture has boiled for approximately for five minutes. Add one teaspoon vanilla, crisp rice cereal, and pecans, if desired, to the mixture while still hot. Allow to cool until easy to handle and roll into balls. Dredge with coconut and leave to cool at room temperature.

Hint: May be frozen.

Yield: 24 balls.

QUICK CHEWY BAR COOKIES

2 cups biscuit mix
1 (16 ounce) box dark brown sugar
4 eggs
1 cup nuts

Grease an 11 X 13 inch pan. Preheat oven to 350°. Mix all ingredients together and pour into greased pan. Bake 15 to 20 minutes.

Hint: A very moist and chewy bar that may be iced with any chocolate icing or with chocolate chips poured on while warm and then spread when melted.

Yield: 20 squares.

TWEETY'S FAMOUS COOKIES

1 cup margarine
1 cup sugar
1 cup brown sugar
2 eggs
2 cups flour
1 teaspoon baking soda
½ teaspoon baking powder
½ teaspoon salt
½ teaspoon cinnamon
2 cups old-fashioned oatmeal
1 teaspoon vanilla
1 (6 ounce) package semi-sweet chocolate chips
Pecans or walnuts, if desired

Measure out the flour, baking soda, baking powder, salt and cinnamon into a bowl. Set aside. Cream the margarine, sugar, brown sugar, and eggs together by hand. Add in the flour mixture and mix. Mix in the oatmeal and vanilla. Add in chocolate chips and nuts, if desired. Use a small ice cream scooper to shape cookie dough. Bake at 350° for 8 to 10 minutes.

Yield: 5 dozen.

APRICOT JUMBLES

2 tablespoons butter
1 cup dried apricots, chopped
2 eggs
1 cup sugar
1 teaspoon vanilla
½ cup nuts, chopped
1 cup coconut
1 cup crushed graham crackers

Melt butter in skillet. Stir in apricots. Beat eggs well. Blend in sugar, add to apricot mixture. Cook over low heat for 15 minutes, stirring constantly. Remove from heat, stir in vanilla, nuts, coconut, and crushed graham crackers. Drop by teaspoon onto waxed paper.

Yield: 4 dozen 1 inch balls.

PUMPKIN-CHOCOLATE CHIP COOKIES

1 cup shortening
1 cup sugar
1 large egg
1 cup canned pumpkin
2 cups flour
1 teaspoon baking soda
1 teaspoon baking powder
½ teaspoon salt
1 teaspoon cinnamon
1 teaspoon vanilla
1 (6 ounce) package chocolate chips
½ cup chopped pecans

Beat shortening until fluffy. Add sugar and beat well. Add egg and pumpkin and mix well. Combine flour and next four ingredients. Add to pumpkin mixture. Stir in vanilla, chocolate chips, and pecans. Drop by tablespoon onto lightly greased cookie sheet. Bake at 350° for 13 minutes. Place on wire rack to cool.

Yield: 3 dozen.

NO BAKE CHOCOLATE OATMEAL DROP COOKIES

½ cup butter or margarine
2 cups sugar
½ cup cocoa
½ cup evaporated milk
2 teaspoons vanilla
3 cups 1-minute oats
1 cup chopped pecans

Combine butter or margarine, sugar, cocoa, and milk in a medium sized saucepan. Bring to a boil and cook for 1 minute. Take off stove and add vanilla, oats, and nuts. Stir until well mixed. Drop cookie mixture onto waxed paper using a tablespoon. Let cool until firm.

Yield: 3 dozen.

DRIED CRANBERRY AND WHITE CHOCOLATE BISCOTTI

2½ cups all-purpose flour
1 teaspoon baking powder
½ teaspoon salt
1½ cups sugar
½ cup unsalted butter, room temperature
2 large eggs
½ teaspoon almond extract
1½ cups dried cranberries
1 egg white
6 ounces high quality white chocolate

Preheat oven to 350°. Line heavy large baking sheet with parchment paper. Combine flour, baking powder, and salt in a medium bowl, whisk to blend. Using electric mixer, beat sugar, butter, 2 eggs, and almond extract in a large bowl until blended. Mix in flour mixture and then dried cranberries. Divide dough in half. Using floured hands, shape each piece into 2½ X 9½ inch long, and 1 inch high logs. Transfer both logs to prepared baking sheet, spacing evenly. Whisk egg white in small bowl until foamy; brush egg white glaze on top and sides of each log. Bake logs until golden brown (logs will spread) about 35 minutes. Cool completely on sheet on wire rack. Maintain oven temperature. Transfer logs to work surface. Discard parchment. Using serrated knife, cut long diagonally into ½ inch wide slices. Arrange slices, cut side down, on same sheet. Bake 10 minutes, turn biscotti over. Bake until just beginning to color, about 5 minutes. Transfer biscotti to rack. Melt chocolate in top of double boiler over simmering water until smooth. Remove from over water. Using a fork, drizzle chocolate over biscotti. Let stand until chocolate sets, about 30 minutes.

Yield: 2 dozen.

LEMON SQUARES

- **2 cups flour, sifted**
- **1 cup warm melted butter**
- **½ cup powdered sugar**
- **2 cups granulated sugar**
- **¼ teaspoons salt**
- **2 lemons**
- **1 teaspoon baking powder**
- **4 eggs, beaten**
- **Additional powdered sugar to sprinkle over finished squares**

Cream together flour, butter, and confectioners' sugar and spread onto a greased 9 X 13 x 2 inch pan. Press in hard and bake for 20 minutes at 350°. Mix the granulated sugar, salt, juice and rind of lemons, baking powder, and eggs. Pour the mixture over the baked crust and bake for 20 to 25 minutes until the top is light brown. Sift powdered sugar over all and cut into small squares.

Yield: 25 to 30 squares.

LEMON CURD

- **½ cup fresh lemon juice (about 4 lemons)**
- **2 cups sugar**
- **¾ cup butter**
- **4 eggs, well beaten**

Combine lemon juice, sugar and butter in a saucepan. Over low heat, cook until sugar is dissolved and butter is melted. Stir hot mixture into well-beaten eggs. Return to heat, stirring constantly until sauce is thickened and coats the spoon. Serve warm or cool. Refrigerate in quart jar until needed.

Yield: 3 cups.

WHITE CHOCOLATE-MACADAMIA CHUNK COOKIES

½ cup butter or margarine at cool room temperature
½ cup sugar
¼ cup firmly packed brown sugar
1 teaspoon vanilla
1 egg
1 cup all-purpose flour
½ teaspoon baking soda
¼ teaspoon salt
8 ounces white chocolate, chopped into large ½ inch chunks
1 (3½ ounce) jar of salted macadamia nuts, coarsely chopped

Beat butter, sugars, vanilla and egg until light and fluffy. Mix flour with soda and salt, blend into butter mixture. Stir in white chocolate chunks and nuts. Chill 1 hour. Drop 2 inches apart by heaping teaspoonfuls onto ungreased baking sheets. Bake at 350° for 12 to 15 minutes, or until lightly browned. Cool 2 minutes before removing from sheets.

Yield: 2 dozen 3 inch cookies.

BRITTLE CRACKER COOKIES

40 saltine crackers
1 cup butter
1 cup brown sugar
1 (6 ounce) package chocolate chips
1 cup chopped nuts

Preheat oven to 350°. Place a layer of aluminum foil in an 11 X 16 inch pan and arrange a single layer of crackers over the foil. Combine butter and brown sugar in a saucepan. Bring to a boil and boil 3 minutes. Pour over crackers. Bake 5 minutes or until crackers float. Remove from oven and sprinkle chocolate chips over top. When melted, spread and sprinkle nuts on top. Cut into bars, following the form of the crackers.

Yield: 24 pieces.

AUNT LINDA ADE'S GINGER COOKIES

¾ cup shortening
1 cup sugar
1 egg
¼ cup molasses
2⅛ cups flour
¼ teaspoon salt
2 teaspoons baking soda
½ teaspoon each cinnamon, ginger and ground cloves
Granulated sugar

Cream the shortening and sugar together until light and fluffy. Beat the egg and molasses well and add to the shortening mixture. Sift together the dry ingredients (except sugar) and add to the shortening mixture. Chill the dough one hour. Roll by hand into 1 inch balls, then roll in granulated sugar. Place the balls 2 inches apart on ungreased cookie sheets. Bake at 375° for 5 to 10 minutes or until lightly browned. Cool slightly, then remove from the baking sheets with a spatula.

Yield: 4 dozen.

ABSOLUTELY WONDERFUL SAND TARTS

½ cup butter, softened
3 tablespoons powdered sugar
1 tablespoon cold water
1½ cups flour
1 teaspoon vanilla
1½ cups pecans, chopped
Additional powdered sugar to roll cookies in

Mix butter with powdered sugar. Add water. Add flour, vanilla, and pecans. Roll cookies about the size of a pecan and bake 30 minutes at 250°. When done, roll cookies in powdered sugar.

Variation: Instead of rolling them in powdered sugar after baking, top each cookie with raspberry jam.

Yield: 2 dozen.

SNOWFLAKE SPRITZ COOKIES

2½ cups sifted all-purpose flour
½ teaspoon salt
¼ teaspoon cinnamon
1 cup butter or margarine
1 (3 ounce) package cream cheese
1 cup sugar
1 egg yolk, unbeaten
1 teaspoon vanilla

Grease cookie sheets. Measure flour, salt and cinnamon into sifter and set aside. Cream butter or margarine and cream cheese until soft. Add sugar gradually, creaming well after each addition. Beat in egg yolk and vanilla. Sift dry ingredients, add and blend well. Pack dough into cookie press design forming plate. Press dough onto prepared cookie sheets. Bake at 350° for 15 to 18 minutes, or until edges are light brown.

Hint: When using cookie press, press nose of press on cookie sheet, then release gun. This makes it much easier.

Yield: 7 dozen.

BROWNIES

5 squares semi-sweet chocolate
½ cup butter
4 eggs
2 cups sugar
1 cup all-purpose flour
1 teaspoon baking powder
½ cup chopped walnuts, optional

Melt chocolate and butter on top of double boiler or in microwave. Cool. Beat eggs and sugar with wooden spoon. Stir in chocolate mixture. Stir in flour, baking powder and nuts, if desired. Bake in greased 8 inch pan in a 350° oven for 30 minutes or until top becomes dull.

Hint: These brownies are not as sweet as some other recipes.

Yield: 12 servings.

CRÈME DE MENTHE BROWNIES

1 cup sugar
1 cup plus 6 tablespoons softened butter, divided
4 eggs
1 (16 ounce) can chocolate syrup
1 cup flour
½ teaspoon salt
1 teaspoon vanilla
2 cups powdered sugar
3 tablespoons green crème de menthe or peppermint flavoring and green food coloring
1 (6 ounce) package chocolate chips

Mix sugar, ½ cup butter, eggs, chocolate syrup, flour, salt, and vanilla together and pour into a 9 X 13 X 2 inch greased pan. Bake at 350° oven for 25 minutes. Cool completely. Cream powdered sugar, ½ cup butter, and crème de menthe with electric mixer until very smooth. Spread over the cooled chocolate layer. Melt the 6 tablespoons butter and chocolate chips. Beat until smooth and pour over the crème de menthe layer. When frosting is set, cut into squares.

Yield: 36 bars.

CLUB CRACKER CRUNCH

Club crackers, salted
½ pound butter
⅔ cup sugar
Slivered almonds

Line (2) 9 X 12 inch jelly-roll or cake pans with heavy duty aluminum foil, going up the sides ½ inch. Arrange crackers close together on top of foil. Put butter and sugar in saucepan and boil 3 minutes. Let mixture come to a boil before timing. Pour hurriedly over crackers, being careful to cover all the crackers. Sprinkle slivered almonds over crackers. Bake at 350° for 8 to 10 minutes. Let cool completely before breaking apart.

Yield: 12 squares.

TEXAS BROWNIES

Cake

2 cups all-purpose flour
2 cups sugar
½ cup butter
½ cup vegetable shortening
1 cup brewed coffee
¼ cup dark, unsweetened cocoa
½ cup buttermilk (or add 2 teaspoons vinegar to ½ cup milk)
2 eggs
1 teaspoon baking soda
1 teaspoon vanilla

Frosting

½ cup butter
2 tablespoons dark, unsweetened cocoa
¼ cup milk
3½ cups unsifted powdered sugar
1 teaspoon vanilla

In large bowl, mix flour and sugar. In saucepan, combine butter, shortening, coffee and cocoa. Stir and heat to boiling. Pour boiling mixture over flour and sugar. Add buttermilk, eggs, baking soda and vanilla. Mix well. Pour into well greased 11 X 17 inch jelly-roll pan. Bake at 400° for 20 minutes or until center is done. While brownies bake, make frosting. In saucepan, bring butter, cocoa, and milk to boil, stirring constantly. Mix in powdered sugar and vanilla and stir until frosting is smooth. Pour warm frosting over brownies as soon as you take them out of oven. Cool.

Yield: 48 squares.

RIENZI'S BROWNIES WITH FUDGE ICING

BROWNIES

2 squares unsweetened chocolate
⅓ cup butter
1 teaspoon vanilla
2 eggs, beaten
⅔ cup flour
1 cup sugar
¼ teaspoon salt
½ teaspoon baking powder
1 cup chopped nuts

ICING

2 squares unsweetened chocolate
2 cups powdered sugar
½ teaspoon salt
2 tablespoons light corn syrup
⅔ cup milk
1 tablespoon butter
1 teaspoon vanilla extract

To prepare brownies, in a small saucepan, melt chocolate and butter together. Cool. Add vanilla and mix in beaten eggs. Sift flour, salt, baking powder, and sugar together. Combine chocolate mixture with dry ingredients. Add nuts. Place in a greased 8 X 8 inch baking pan. Bake in a preheated 375° oven until edges are firm. Take out of oven and mix firm edges into soft center portion, then spread out evenly again (this will make the finished brownies moist and chewy). Return pan to oven and bake for about 5 more minutes. Turn oven to broil and heat until top is firm. Cool before frosting. To prepare icing, combine sugar, salt, chocolate, syrup, and milk in saucepan. Mix well and cook for 5 to 10 minutes on medium heat, stirring continuously. Add butter and vanilla. Beat to a satiny finish and spreadable consistency.

Yield: 12 squares.

CARAMEL CHOCOLATE SQUARES

50 light caramels
⅔ cup evaporated milk, divided
1 package German chocolate cake mix
⅔ cup melted margarine
⅓ cup chopped nuts
1 cup dark chocolate chips

In heavy saucepan, combine caramels and ⅓ cup evaporated milk. Heat until melted. Set aside. Grease a 9 X 13 X 2 inch pan. In large bowl, combine dry cake mix, melted margarine, ⅓ cup evaporated milk, and nuts. Stir by hand until dough sticks together. Press half the dough into pan, reserve other half. Bake at 350° for 8 minutes. While hot, spread the caramel mixture on top. Spread chocolate chips over the top of the caramel layer. Crumble the rest of the cake mixture on top. Return to oven and bake 20 minutes longer. Refrigerate for 30 minutes. Cut into small squares.

Yield: 24 servings.

FROZEN LEMON MOUSSE

4 eggs, separated
1 cup sugar, divided
1½ tablespoons finely grated lemon zest
½ cup fresh lemon juice
1½ cup heavy whipping cream
Fresh berries puréed, for garnish

Beat egg whites until stiff. Gradually add ¾ cup sugar, 1 tablespoon at a time. Beat until stiff and glossy. In another bowl, beat egg yolks and remaining ¼ cup sugar until light and creamy. Add lemon juice and zest. Whip cream until stiff. Fold egg whites, yolks, and cream together using a rubber spatula. Pour into large serving dish or individual glasses. Freeze at least 8 hours, well covered. Cover with berry purée, if desired.

Yield: 60 ounces or 12 (5 ounce) cups.

PUMPKIN ICE CREAM PIE

Filling

1 cup canned pumpkin
½ cup brown sugar
½ teaspoon salt
½ teaspoon cinnamon
½ teaspoon ginger
¼ teaspoon nutmeg
1 quart vanilla ice cream, softened

Crust

12-14 graham crackers, finely crumbled
¼ cup sugar
¼ cup butter

To make crust, combine graham crackers, sugar, and butter. Pat into a 9 inch pie pan. Bake for 10 minutes at 350°. Chill before filling. To prepare filling, combine all ingredients with the softened (but not melted) ice cream. Pour into crust. Freeze pie before serving.

Variation: Add whipped cream and/or crushed peanut brittle to the top of pie.

Yield: 8 servings.

PEACH MARLOW

20 marshmallows
1 cup fresh crushed peaches
¼ cup water
3 tablespoons sugar
½ pint whipping cream

Sprinkle peaches with sugar. Let stand while marshmallows and water are melting in the top of a double boiler. When liquid, add peaches and chill in refrigerator. When cool, add already whipped cream and freeze. Set out 5 minutes before serving.

Yield: 8 servings.

PEARS IN RED WINE

5 medium to large Bartlett pears (about 1½ pounds), peeled, quartered, and cored
1½ cups hearty red wine
⅓ cup sugar
Grated rind of 1 lemon
¼ cup lemon juice

Place the pears, wine, sugar, lemon rind and lemon juice in a large saucepan. Bring the mixture to a boil, reduce the heat to low, cover and boil the mixture gently for about 25 minutes (less if the pears are very ripe, more if they are unripe or if a harder variety is used). Pierce the pears with the point of a sharp knife to determine tenderness. Using a slotted spoon, transfer the pears to a serving bowl, reserving liquid. You should have about 1¼ cups of liquid. Bring it to a boil and boil it until it is reduced to about ⅔ cup. Add it to the pears and cool to room temperature. (The liquid should become syrupy). Divide the pear quarters among 6 small, deep dessert dishes. Spoon syrup over and serve.

Yield: 6 servings.

SWEET KUGEL

16 ounces wide egg noodles
1 cup cottage cheese
1 cup sour cream
5 eggs, beaten
½ cup butter, melted
¾ cup honey
2 tablespoons cinnamon
½ teaspoon salt

Cook noodles and drain. Add all the ingredients and put in an 9 X 13 X 2 inch greased baking dish. Sprinkle cinnamon over the kugel and bake for 50 to 60 minutes at 350°.

Yield: 12 servings.

WHITE WINE GRANITA WITH BLACKBERRIES

1 bottle sweet white wine
½ cup sugar
4 tablespoons juniper berries
4 cinnamon sticks
2 pints blackberries

Bring wine and sugar to boil over high heat, stirring once or twice. Meanwhile, wrap juniper berries loosely in plastic wrap and crush with a rolling pin. Add to wine syrup with cinnamon sticks and let simmer 5 to 7 minutes. Pick over berries and chill, uncovered. Rinse only if necessary, just before serving. Strain infused syrup into a shallow glass baking dish, cover with plastic wrap and chill in freezer until firm and lightly crystallized, about 3 hours. You can leave it up to 12 hours in the freezer. Chill glasses. Just before serving, pile berries in chilled glasses. With a fork, scrape granita into soft chunks and pile on fruit. Serve at once with cookies on side.

Yield: 8 servings.

SHERRIED FRUIT COMPOTE

1 apple, sliced
1 cup chunk pineapple
2 peaches, sliced
3 fresh, peeled apricots or 1 medium can
1 pear, sliced
½ cup margarine
½ cup brown sugar
2 tablespoons flour
1 cup sherry

Alternate different kinds of fruit in layers in a 9 X 12 inch pan. Combine margarine, brown sugar, flour, and sherry in top of a double boiler. Cook until thick and smooth. Pour over fruit. Cover and let stand several hours. Cook at 350° for 20 to 25 minutes.

Variation: Add ¼ to ½ teaspoon nutmeg or 1 teaspoon curry powder.

Yield: 8 servings.

CHOCOLATE MERINGUES

MERINGUES

- 4 **egg whites**
- 1½ **cups sugar**
- ¼ **teaspoon cream of tartar**
- ¼ **teaspoon almond extract**

FILLING

- 2 **egg whites**
- ½ **cup sugar**
- 2 **tablespoons cocoa**
- ¾ **cup butter**
- 4 **ounces of semi-sweet chocolate chips, melted**
- 1 **cube of almond bark, vanilla flavored**
- ½ **cup ground almonds**

To prepare meringues, beat egg whites to stiff peak stage, adding cream of tartar and almond extract. While the mixer is still on, slowly add the sugar, one teaspoon at a time, until mixture is stiff. From brown paper, cut 36 rounds about 3 inches in diameter. Spread each round with meringue, making a slight ring around the edges. Place on a cookie sheet and bake 10 minutes at 300°. Turn off heat and let meringues dry 5 minutes longer.

To prepare filling, beat egg whites, sugar and cocoa in top of a double boiler over hot (not boiling) water until smooth. Still beating constantly, add the butter by spoonfuls and add the melted sweet chocolate and shaved almond bark. Remove from the heat, stirring occasionally, until the mixture is spreading consistency. Swirl the filling into the "nest" of the meringues and sprinkle the tops with ground nuts.

Hint: This recipe freezes nicely. Remove 30 minutes before serving.

Yield: 36 pieces.

OREGON BLACKBERRY MERINGUE CUPS

3½ cups blackberries, divided
½ cup sugar, divided
¾ cup plain lowfat yogurt
½ teaspoon grated lemon peel
3 large egg whites
Mint sprigs

In a small bowl combine ½ cup blackberries and 1 tablespoon sugar. Set aside. In another bowl, combine 2 tablespoons sugar, yogurt, and lemon peel. Gently mix in remaining berries. Spoon yogurt/berry mixture into 4 oven-proof ramekins or bowls. Suggested bowl size should be 1½ to 2 inches deep by 4 to 5 inches wide. In deep bowl, whip egg whites with mixer at high speed until foamy. Continue to beat and gradually add remaining sugar (about 1 tablespoon every 15 seconds), until whites hold stiff peaks when beaters are lifted. Swirl meringue equally over yogurt/berry mixture. Set dishes in 10 X 15 inch rimmed pan. Broil about 4 inches from heat until meringue is browned (about 30 to 60 seconds). Spoon reserved sugared berries and their juice over meringues. Garnish with mint sprigs.

Variation: Brandy or liqueur may be added to berries used as the topping.

Yield: 4 servings.

AUNT EDITH'S CHOCOLATE SAUCE

2 squares unsweetened baking chocolate
2 tablespoons unsalted butter
1 cup sugar
½ cup water
1 teaspoon vanilla

Melt the butter and chocolate in saucepan over low heat. Add 1 cup sugar and ½ cup water at the same time. Stir and bring to a boil. Boil 7 minutes or until syrup consistency. Add 1 teaspoon vanilla. Cool slightly. Put over ice cream.

Yield: 1½ cups.

MERINGUE FORGETUMS

2 egg whites
⅔ cup sugar
Pinch of salt
1 teaspoon vanilla
1 cup chopped nuts
⅓ cup chocolate bits, optional

Preheat oven to 350°. Beat egg whites until stiff but not dry. Add sugar one tablespoon at a time, continue beating. Add salt and vanilla. Fold in nuts and chocolate bits, if desired. Drop by teaspoon onto ungreased cookie sheet. Turn off oven. Make at night and leave in oven overnight. Store in airtight container or sealed plastic bag.

Yield: 2 to 3 dozen.

CHEWY PECAN PIE SQUARES

1 package yellow cake mix
5 eggs, divided
⅓ cup oil
1 cup light corn syrup
2 tablespoons margarine
1 teaspoon vanilla
2 cups chopped pecans

Heat oven to 350°. Grease a 9 X 13 X 2-inch pan. Combine cake mix, 1 egg and oil until crumbly. Press into bottom of pan. Bake 15 minutes or less. Do not brown. Beat remaining 4 eggs, syrup and melted margarine until blended. Do not overbeat. Add pecans and pour onto crust. Bake for 30 minutes at 325° until filling is set in the center. Completely cool before cutting into squares.

Yield: 24 pieces.

SWEET WONTON "NAPOLEON"

24 ounces nonfat frozen vanilla or strawberry yogurt
About 2 tablespoons confectioners' sugar
24 ripe strawberries (about 2 pints), washed, hulled and quartered lengthwise
18 (3 inch square) wonton wrappers

Preheat oven to 375°. Bring about 2 quarts of water to a boil in a large pot. Add 9 of the wonton wrappers, dropping them into the water 1 at a time. Cook for 1½ minutes, then remove them from the water carefully with a skimmer and transfer them to a large bowl of cold water. Lightly coat a 16 X 14 inch cookie sheet with vegetable cooking spray. Place your hands in the bowl containing the wrappers and carefully unfold them 1 at a time under the water. Transfer them, still wet, to the cookie sheet, arranging them side by side. Lightly spray the surface with more cooking spray. Bake for 16 to 18 minutes, or until dry and brown. Transfer the crisped wrappers to a cake rack to cool. Cover after baking to keep pliable. Repeat with the remaining wonton wrappers. Using 3 crisps for each serving, assemble each dessert as follows: Place a wonton crisp on a dessert plate and top it with a flattened 2 ounce scoop of the yogurt. Place another wonton crisp on top of the yogurt, positioning it at about a 45 degree angle in relation to the first crisp. Add a second flattened 2 ounce scoop of the yogurt. Cap with the third wonton crisp. Sprinkle the top crisp with 1 teaspoon of powdered sugar and decorate the dessert with the equivalent of 4 berries. A stunning dessert.

Yield: 6 servings.

SWEDISH NUT BALLS

1 cup chopped pecans
1 cup all-purpose flour
½ cup butter
2 tablespoons sugar
⅛ teaspoon salt
1 teaspoon vanilla
Powdered sugar for rolling

Mix ingredients well. Form into walnut size balls. Bake in a preheated 275° oven for 30 minutes. Roll in powdered sugar while hot and again when cool.

Yield: 24 balls.

FROZEN CHERRY CREAM

- **1 (14 ounce) can condensed milk**
- **1 cup cherry pie filling**
- **1 (12 ounce) can crushed pineapple, undrained**
- **¼ cup lemon juice**
- **½ teaspoon almond extract**
- **1 pint whipping cream**

Mix first five ingredients together well. Prepare whipping cream. Fold whipped cream into mixture. Pour into an 8 X 12 inch pan. Put in freezer for 24 hours. Cut into small squares.

Yield: 12 to 18 servings.

FUDGE SAUCE FOR ICE CREAM

- **1 cup granulated sugar**
- **2 tablespoons cocoa**
- **2 tablespoons butter**
- **1 cup evaporated milk**
- **1 teaspoon vanilla**

Combine sugar and cocoa and stir over low heat about 2 minutes. Do not let the sugar melt. Add butter and keep stirring, add milk stirring constantly. Increase heat and boil rapidly for 3 minutes while stirring. Remove from heat and add vanilla. Serve hot or cold.

Yield: 1½ cups.

"RAVO"

2 tablespoons melted butter
2 tablespoons semolina
2 tablespoons sugar
2 cups milk
1 tablespoon seedless raisins
¼ teaspoon mixed cardamom and nutmeg powder
15 almonds, blanched and finely sliced

Heat butter and add semolina. Cook, stirring, until semolina is slightly fried and pale gold in color. Add sugar and milk and keep stirring until mixture thickens. Pour into a shallow dish or pie plate and allow to cool and set. Sprinkle with powdered cardamom and nutmeg, raisins and almonds and serve.

Yield: 4 servings.

ORANGE SOUFFLÉ

2 envelopes unflavored gelatin
2 cups sugar
4 egg yolks
2½ cups orange juice, divided
3 tablespoons fresh lemon juice
1 cup mandarin orange sections
2 cups heavy cream, whipped to soft peaks

Soften gelatin in ½ cup of the orange juice. Set aside. Combine sugar, egg yolks, and 1 cup orange juice. Cook over low heat until mixture is steaming and slightly thickened. Do not boil. Add the gelatin, the remaining orange juice, and the lemon juice. Transfer the custard to a clean mixing bowl. Immerse the bowl into a larger bowl filled with ice and water. Cool the custard, stirring occasionally, until syrupy. Gently fold cream into custard mix, until no streaks remain. Place the orange sections in the bottom of a 2 quart ring mold, or in 12 individual molds. Fill molds with the orange soufflé. Chill until firm, about 2 hours.

Yield: 12 servings.

Cooking Tips & Index

Camille Pissarro, French, 1830-1903
The Vegetable Market at Pontoise, 1891
Etching and aquatint, plate 9 15/16 x 7 3/4 in., sheet 11 13/16 x 10 1/16 in.
The Museum of Fine Arts, Houston, museum purchase with funds provided by the 1991 Prints and Drawing Benefit

Although typically Impressionist subject matter dealt with the urban pleasures of the bourgeoisie, Camille Pissarro more often depicted the harsher life of the peasants. Pissarro, unlike most of his colleagues, lived and worked in the then rural outskirts of Paris, first at Pontoise, where he lived from 1866 to 1882. In this image, he depicts the weekly vegetable market where the farmers brought the produce they had raised directly to the urban consumers, a once important aspect of French life that has all but disappeared.

Cooking Tips

Stuff a miniature marshmallow in the bottom of a sugar cone to prevent ice cream drips.

Use lifesaver candy to hold candles in place on your next birthday cake.

Use a meat baster to "squeeze" your pancake batter onto the hot griddle-perfect shaped pancakes every time.

If you have problems opening jars try using latex dishwashing gloves or large rubber bands wrapped around the lid. They give a non-slip grip that makes opening jars easy.

Push a drinking straw to the bottom of the ketchup bottle and remove. This admits enough air to start the ketchup flowing.

Wrap celery in aluminum foil when putting in the refrigerator and it will keep for weeks.

Store tomatoes at room temperature with stems pointed downward and they will retain their flavor and freshness longer.

Ice cold water will keep apples from turning brown.

Avocados will ripen faster if placed in tightly closed brown paper sack and left to sit out for a day or two.

Popcorn should always be stored in the freezer. Not only will it stay fresh, but freezing helps eliminate "old maids" or kernels that won't pop.

When boiling corn on the cob, add a pinch of sugar to help bring out the corn's natural sweetness.

To get 1 cup of fruit pulp from dried fruit, bring 1½ cups water and 1½ cups dried fruit to a boil. Reduce heat and continue cooking until the liquid is gone. Mash fruit if desired.

Don't throw out leftover wine. Freeze in ice cubes for future use in casseroles and sauces.

To get the most juice out of fresh lemons, bring them to room temperature and roll them under your palm against the kitchen counter.

Freeze the juice from canned tomatoes in ice cube trays. When frozen, store in plastic bags in freezer for cooking or for tomato juice based drinks.

Before placing ham in the roasting pan, slit rind lengthwise on the underside. The rind will peel away as the ham cooks, and can be easily removed.

If you accidentally over-salt a dish while it's still cooking drop in a peeled potato, it absorbs the excess salt for an instant "fix."

You can tell a whole chicken is done when a meat thermometer placed at the inner thigh registers 180 degrees F. Boneless, skinless chicken is done when the meat is no longer pink and the juices run clear when the meat is pierced.

Cheese is easier to grate if it is cold. Any hard natural cheese may be grated in a blender if it is cut into small cubes and dropped in blender a handful at a time.

Zap garlic cloves in the microwave for 15 seconds and the skins slip right off.

For quick and handy seasoning, keep a large shaker containing both salt and pepper.

Rice will be fluffier if 1 teaspoon of lemon juice is added to water in which rice is cooked.

To keep frying food from spattering, invert a metal colander over the pan, allowing steam to escape.

Add a teaspoon of butter or a few teaspoons of cooking oil to boiling pasta water. Rice, noodles or spaghetti will not boil over or stick together.

To keep potatoes from budding, place an apple in the bag with the potatoes.

Overcooked potatoes can become soggy when milk is added. Sprinkle with dry powdered milk for the fluffiest mashed potatoes ever.

To hurry up baked potatoes, boil in salted water for 10 minutes, and then place in a very hot oven. Or cut potatoes in half and place them face down on baking sheet.

Substitution Chart for Casserole Pans

4 Cups	=	9" pie plate 8" x 1¼" layer cake pan 7⅜" x 3⅝" x 2¼" loaf pan
6 Cups	=	10" pie plate 9" x 1½" layer cake pan 8½" x 3⅝" x 2⅝" loaf pan
8 Cups	=	8" x 8" x 2" square pan 9" x 5" x 3" loaf pan 11" x 7" x 1½" baking pan
10 Cups	=	9" x 9" x 2" square pan 11¾" x 7½" x 1¾" baking pan 15" x 10" x 1" jelly-roll pan
12 Cups	=	13½" x 8½" x 2" glass baking pan
15 Cups	=	13" x 9" x 2" metal baking pan
16 Cups	=	13" x 9" x 3" roasting pan
19 Cups	=	14" x 10½" x 2½" roasting pan

Liquid Measure Equivalents

dash	=	less than ⅛ teaspoon
1 teaspoon	=	⅓ tablespoon
1 tablespoon	=	3 teaspoons
2 tablespoons	=	1 fluid ounce
4 tablespoons	=	¼ cup or 2 fluid ounces
8 tablespoons	=	½ cup, 4 fluid ounces or 1 gill
16 tablespoons	=	1 cup, 8 fluid ounces or ½ pint

¼ cup	=	4 tablespoons
⅓ cup	=	5 tablespoons plus 1 teaspoon
⅜ cup	=	¼ cup plus 2 tablespoons
½ cup	=	8 tablespoons
⅝ cup	=	½ cup plus 2 tablespoons
⅔ cup	=	10 tablespoons plus 2 teaspoons
¾ cup	=	12 tablespoons
⅞ cup	=	¾ cups plus 2 tablespoons
1 cup	=	8 fluid ounces or ½ pint
2 cups	=	16 fluid ounces or 1 pint
4 cups	=	2 pints or 1 quart
16 cups	=	8 pints, 4 quarts or 1 gallon

Ingredient Substitutions for Baking

1 teaspoon **baking powder**
= ¼ teaspoon baking soda, ½ teaspoon cream of tartar

1 cup **butter**
= ⅞ cup vegetable oil or shortening

1 oz. square **unsweetened chocolate**
= 3½ tablespoons cocoa, ½ tablespoon butter

1⅔ oz. **Semi-sweet chocolate**
= 1 oz. Unsweetened chocolate, 4 teaspoons sugar

2 tablespoons **flour**
= 1 tablespoon cornstarch

1 cup sifted **all-purpose flour**
= 1 cup and 2 tablespoons sifted cake flour

1 cup **whole milk**
= ½ cup evaporated milk, ½ cup water

1 cup **sour milk**
= 1 cup milk, 1 tablespoon vinegar or lemon juice

1 cup **sour cream**
= ⅞ cup buttermilk or sour milk, 3 tablespoons butter

1 cup **sour cream**
= 1 cup plain yogurt

1 teaspoon **sugar**
= ⅛ teaspoon noncaloric sweetener

1 cup **sugar**
= ½ cup maple syrup, ¼ cup corn syrup
(lessen liquid in recipe by 2 tablespoons)

1 cup **sugar**
= 1 cup honey (lessen liquid in recipe by ¼ cup)

1 cup **light brown sugar**
= 1 cup granulated sugar, ¼ cup unsulphured light molasses

1 cup **dark brown sugar**
= 1 cup granulated sugar, ½ cup unsulphured light molasses

Herb, Spice, Fruit and Vegetable Equivalents

Apples (1 pound)	= 3 cups pared and sliced
Apricots, dried (1 pound)	= 3¼ cups, 5½ lbs. fresh, 3 cups cooked
Bananas, 3 to 4 medium (1 pound)	= 1¾ cups mashed
Bay leaf, whole	= ¼ teaspoon crushed
Cabbage, head (1 pound)	= 6 cups minced, 4½ cups shredded
Carrots (1 pound)	= 2½ cups diced, 3 cups shredded
Garlic, small clove	= ⅛ teaspoon powdered
Ginger, raw (1 tablespoon)	= ⅛ teaspoon powdered
Herbs, fresh (1 tablespoon)	= ⅓ to ½ teaspoon dried
Horseradish, prepared (2 tablespoons)	= 1 tablespoon grated
Lemon, medium	= 2-3 tablespoons juice 1¼ teaspoons grated rind (½ teaspoon extract)
Lemon juice (1 teaspoon)	= ½ teaspoon vinegar
Mushrooms, fresh (1 pound)	= 3 ounces dried, 12 ounces canned
Mustard, prepared (1 tablespoon)	= 1 teaspoon dry or powdered
Orange, medium	= 6-8 tablespoons juice ¾ cup diced, 2 to 3 tablespoons grated rind (teaspoon extract)
Peaches, 4 medium (1 pound)	= 2 cups sliced
Pepper, large green (6 ounces)	= 1 cup diced
Potatoes, 3 medium raw (1 pound)	= 3½ to 4 cups sliced
Potatoes, cooked (1 pound)	= 2¼ cups, 1¾ cups mashed
Prunes, dried (1 pound)	= 2¼ cups pitted, 2 cups cooked
Raisins, seedless (1 pound)	= 2¾ cups

A

Absolutely Wonderful Sand Tarts 223
Aimee's Artichoke and
Sun-Dried Tomato Dip 21
Aimee's Bombay Chiller 73
Akuri Spiced Scrambled Eggs 65
Alison's Salmon 183

ALMONDS, *see Nuts*

Amy's Brie Soup 78

APPETIZERS *(also see Dips and Spreads)*
Alexander's Smoked Salmon
or Ham Roll-Ups 38
Asparagus Appetizers 22
Baked Spinach Square 28
Caviar Pie 19
Cheese Straws 39
Ham-Asparagus Roll-Ups 22
Jalapeño Cheese Bites 31
Jalapeño Squares 31
Karen's Raspberry Cheese Spread 20
Olive Cheese Nuggets 25
Pastelitos 40
Pickle Mushrooms à la Grecque 24
Pirkko's Caviar 19
Pizza Rustica 32
Shrimp de Jonghe 34
Southwestern Salmon Spirals 35
Texas Caviar 30
Tortilla Roll-Ups 30
Venison Tenderloin Appetizers 42
Zack's Cream Cheese Torte 20
Zucchini Nibbles 23

APPLES
Apple and Red Chili Chutney 161
Apple Bavarian Torte 216
Baked Apple French Toast 65
Dump Coffee Cake 193
Grandma's Apple Crisp 215
Pork Tenderloin with Apple
and Red Chile Chutney 161
Sherried Fruit Compote 231
Applesauce Oat Muffins 53
Apricot Brandy Pound Cake 192

APRICOTS
Apricot Jumbles 218
Apricot Whip 191
Armenian Pilaf 131

ARTICHOKES
Aimee's Artichoke and
Sun-Dried Tomato Dip 21
Artichoke Dip 21
Chicken with Artichokes 168
Creamy Artichoke Soup 75
Greek-Style Chicken and Penne Salad . . . 121
Spinach Casserole 133

ASPARAGUS
Asparagus Appetizers 22
Grilled Asparagus 125
Ham-Asparagus Roll-Ups 22
Savory Chicken and Asparagus 175
Sweet 'n' Sour Asparagus 125
Aunt Edith's Chocolate Sauce 233
Aunt Linda Ade's Ginger Cookies 223

AVOCADO
Diego Rivera Salad 89
Gazpacho with Sour Cream 80
Valerie's Tortilla Soup 85

B

Baked Apple French Toast 65
Baked Brie with Crudités 29
Baked Cushaw 135
Baked Spinach Square 28
Balsamic Dressing 109
Barbara Lea's Chicken Salad 96
Basil Pesto 108
Bean Sprouts, Chicken Sauté
with Fresh Ginger 177

BEANS AND PEAS
Black Bean, Orzo and Tomato Salad . . . 93
Black-Eyed Pea Salad 95
Butch's Wild West Tex-Mex Salad 87
Cajun Veggie Chili 74
Corn Salad 99
Lamb and White Bean Ragoût 164
Nutty Wild Rice Salad 92
Poached Chicken with
Black Beans and Salsa 174
Portuguese Kale Soup 76
Portuguese Soup 77
Tex-Mex Marinated Salad 86
Texas Caviar 30
Virginia's Tomato Aspic 103
White Bean Tuna Salad 96
Béchamel Sauce 151

BEEF
CORNED BEEF
Bob's New York Corned Beef 144
GROUND BEEF
Beef and Cheddar Loaf 149
Chili 147
Eggplant Moussaka 150
Macaroni Pastitsio with
Phyllo Pastry (Pastilla) 152
Moist Meat Loaf 149
Pastelitos 40
Sweet and Sour Cabbage Rolls 153
Texas Stew 146
ROAST
Great Brisket 143
Grillades 156
Standing Rib Roast 141
STEAK
Filet Mignon 143
Flambéed Pepper Steak 145
Teriyaki 144
STEW BEEF
Kathryn's Stew 145
Oven Beef Stew 146
TENDERLOIN
Easy Chateau Stroganoff 142
Beer Bread 56

BEETS
Frosted Beet Soup . . . 79
Greek Salad . . . 91

BELL PEPPERS
Csirke Paprikas Budapest (Chicken Paprika) . . . 179
Eggplant, Red Pepper and Feta Gratin . . . 127
Pepper Jelly . . . 104
Taos Society Soup (Roasted Red Pepper Soup) . . . 83

BEVERAGES
Brandied Mocha . . . 43
Café Brulot . . . 45
Champagne with Raspberries . . . 44
Christmas Tea . . . 45
Cranberry Glogg . . . 50
Eggnog No. 302 . . . 47
Festive Party Punch . . . 46
Ginger Almond Tea . . . 46
Holiday Champagne Punch . . . 44
Hot Gingered Lemonade . . . 43
Jalapeño Margaritas . . . 49
Kentucky Christmas Cider . . . 47
Lemony-Light Cooler . . . 48
Mint Syrup Concentrate . . . 48
Sangría . . . 49
Sparkling Strawberry Punch . . . 50

Black Bean, Orzo and Tomato Salad . . . 93
Black-Eyed Pea Salad . . . 95

BLACKBERRIES
Oregon Blackberry Meringue Cups . . . 233
White Wine Granita with Blackberries . . . 231

Boiled Custard . . . 200
Brandied Cranberry Sauce . . . 105
Brandied Mocha . . . 43
Brandy Alexander Pie . . . 210

BREADS
Applesauce Oat Muffins . . . 53
Baked Apple French Toast . . . 65
Beer Bread . . . 56
Breakfast Meeting Treats . . . 53
Challah French Toast . . . 64
Cheese Bread Rachael . . . 58
Cheese Puffs . . . 62
Fran's Coffee Cake . . . 54
French Coffee Cake . . . 57
Honey Puff . . . 70
Potato Rolls . . . 60
Pumpkin Bread . . . 60
Rick's Waffles . . . 56
Rosemary Damper . . . 61
Spinach Roll . . . 63
Strawberry Bread . . . 61
Sweet Potato Biscuits . . . 59
Zucchini Bread . . . 62

BREAKFAST AND BRUNCH
Akuri Spiced Scrambled Eggs . . . 65
Baked Apple French Toast . . . 65
Breakfast Meeting Treats . . . 53
Challah French Toast . . . 64
Curried Chicken Tea Sandwiches . . . 64
Huevos Rancheros al Pavo . . . 66
Prysnac . . . 66
Quiche without Crust . . . 68
Rick's Waffles . . . 56
Spinach and Mushroom Quiche . . . 69
Swiss Tarts . . . 69

Brittle Cracker Cookies . . . 222

BROCCOLI
Broccoli Cole Slaw . . . 100
Cowboy Cheddar Soup . . . 77
Fettuccine Primavera . . . 115
Pasta with Sun-Dried Tomatoe . . . 116
Prysnac . . . 66
Twice-Cooked Pork with Cabbage and Sai Fun . . . 158

Brownies . . . 224
Butch's Wild West Tex-Mex Salad . . . 87
Buttermilk Glaze Icing . . . 195

C

CABBAGE
Confetti Cole Slaw . . . 100
Fumi Salad . . . 99
Portuguese Soup . . . 77
Sweet and Sour Cabbage Rolls . . . 153

Café Brulot . . . 45
Cajun Veggie Chili . . . 74

CAKES *(also see Candy, Cookies & Bars, Chocolate, Desserts, and Pies)*
Apricot Brandy Pound Cake . . . 192
Black Russian Cake . . . 194
Cake Roll . . . 203
Chocolate Chip Cake . . . 198
Chocolate Delight . . . 199
Dump Coffee Cake . . . 193
Grandma Moses' Gingerbread . . . 196

ICINGS AND FROSTINGS
Buttermilk Glaze Icing . . . 195
Glaze . . . 194
Icing . . . 197

Lady Finger Mousse Cake . . . 199
Masterson Family Frozen Fruitcake . . . 200
Passover Sponge Cake . . . 196
Pumpkin Cake . . . 193
Rhoda's Pound Cake . . . 192
Rose Bowles' Fabulous Fruitcake . . . 201
Seven-Up Cake . . . 201
The Best Cake (Really) . . . 195
The Best Chocolate Cake . . . 197
Vanilla Wafer Cake . . . 198

Calabacitas . . . 134
Calabacitas (Cream of Squash Soup) . . . 80
Canard L'Orange (Roast Duck with Oranges) . . . 180

CANDY *(also see Cakes, Cookies & Bars, Chocolate, Desserts, and Pies)*
Chocolate Mint Bars . . . 208
Cinnamon Pecans . . . 205
Club Cracker Crunch . . . 225
Date Balls . . . 217
Iced Chocolate and Brandy Creams . . . 206
Meringue Forgetums . . . 234
Microwave Chocolate Peanut Clusters . . . 207

Microwave Pecan Brittle 206
Pralines (from Brennan's) 207
Swedish Nut Balls 235
Capanada 36
Caramel Chocolate Squares 228

CARROTS

Carrots in Mustard Dill Sauce 128
Lamb and White Bean Ragoût 164
Oven Beef Stew 146
Portuguese Soup 77

CASSEROLES

Almond Poppy Chicken 171
Calabacitas 134
Chicken Enchiladas 170
Creamy Baked Chicken Breasts 170
Creamy Chicken 175
Easy Chateau Stroganoff 142
Eggplant Moussaka 150
Eggplant, Red Pepper and Feta Gratin . . . 127
Hash Brown Potato Casserole 129
Savory Chicken and Asparagus 175
Spinach and Rice Casserole 133
Spinach Casserole 133
Three Corn Casserole 126
Turnip Soufflé 138
Veal Cutlets Parmesan 154
Vidalia Onion Pie 126
Wild Rice and Cranberry Pilaf 132
Yellow Squash and
Cornbread Casserole 136
Caviar Pie 19
Challah French Toast 64
Champagne with Raspberries 44

CHEESE

4 Star Pasta 119
Aimee's Artichoke and
Sun-Dried Tomato Dip 21
Almond Swiss Cheese Ball 26
Amy's Brie Soup 78
Baked Brie with Crudités 29
Beef and Cheddar Loaf 149
Cheese Bread Rachael 58
Cheese Puffs 62
Cheese Straws 39
Chicken Enchiladas 170
Chicken Pillows for Two 169
Christmas Salad 90
Chutney Cheese Pâté 33
Company's Coming Strata 67
Cowboy Cheddar Soup 77
Creamy Baked Chicken Breasts 170
Curried Cheese and Olive Spread 25
Goat Cheese with Sun-Dried
Tomatoes and Rosemary 27
Gougère with Gruyère Salad 89
Greek Salad 91
Hash Brown Potato Casserole 129
Jalapeño Cheese Bites 31
Jalapeño Squares 31
Karen's Raspberry Cheese Spread 20
Macaroni and Cheese 118
Macaroni Pastitsio with
Phyllo Pastry (Pastilla) 152
Mary Anne Varner's
Rococo Chicken 167
Muenster Chicken 169
Olive Cheese Nuggets 25
Orzo Salad 92
Pasta with Sun-Dried Tomatoe 116
Peter Marzio's Famous Lasagna 148
Pinecone Cheese Ball 26
Pizza Rustica 32
Prysnac 66
Rosemary Damper 61
Sausage and Mostaccioli Bake 118
Savory Chicken and Asparagus 175
Soft Chicken Tacos 178
Southwestern Salmon Spirals 35
Spinach Roll 63
Stuffed Ziti 117
Swiss Tarts 69
Valerie's Tortilla Soup 85
Veal Cutlets Parmesan 154

CHERRIES

Mary Anne Varner's Little Lizzies 202
Rose Bowles' Fabulous Fruitcake 201
Chewy Pecan Pie Squares 234

CHICKEN, *see Poultry*

CHILI

Cajun Veggie Chili 74
Chili 147
Chilled Cucumber Soup 73

CHOCOLATE *(also see Cakes, Candy, Cookies & Bars, Desserts, and Pies)*

Aunt Edith's Chocolate Sauce 233
Brittle Cracker Cookies 222
Brownies 224
Caramel Chocolate Squares 228
Chocolate Chip Cake 198
Chocolate Delight 199
Chocolate Delight Pie 211
Chocolate Meringues 232
Chocolate Mint Bars 208
Chocolate Mint Mousse 208
Crème De Menthe Brownies 225
Dried Cranberry and
White Chocolate Biscotti 220
Fudge Sauce for Ice Cream 236
German Chocolate Angel Pie 212
Helen Corbitt's Grasshopper Pie 213
Iced Chocolate and Brandy Creams 206
Lady Finger Mousse Cake 199
Microwave Chocolate Peanut Clusters 207
Mousse au Chocolat 204
Pumpkin-Chocolate Chip Cookies . . . 219
Rienzi's Brownies with Fudge Icing 227
Texas Brownies 226
The Best Chocolate Cake 197
Tweety's Famous Cookies 218
White Chocolate-
Macadamia Chunk Cookies 222
Christmas Salad 90
Christmas Tea 45
Chutney Cheese Pâté 33
Cinnamon Pecans 205
Club Cracker Crunch 225
Cocktail Sauce 107

COCONUT
Apricot Jumbles 218
Chicken Curry 172
Curried Chicken Tea Sandwiches 64
Debbye's Chicken Log Appetizer 39
Dream Pie 211
French Coffee Cake 57
Hawaiian Chicken Curry 173
Vanilla Wafer Cake 198
Company's Coming Strata 67
CONDIMENTS AND RELISHES
Brandied Cranberry Sauce 105
Cocktail Sauce 107
Cranberry Chutney 107
Fancy Mustard 104
Fresh Cranberry Relish 106
Jezebel Sauce 110
Mango Chutney 110
Marianna's Mustard Sauce 112
Mayonnaise from Rienzi 112
Pepper Jelly 104
Confetti Cole Slaw 100
COOKIES AND BARS *(also see Cakes, Candy, Chocolate, Desserts, and Pies)*
Absolutely Wonderful Sand Tarts 223
Apricot Jumbles 218
Aunt Linda Ade's Ginger Cookies 223
Brittle Cracker Cookies 222
Brownies 224
Caramel Chocolate Squares 228
Chewy Pecan Pie Squares 234
Club Cracker Crunch 225
Crème De Menthe Brownies 225
Dried Cranberry and White Chocolate Biscotti 220
Lemon Squares 221
Mary Anne Varner's Little Lizzies 202
No Bake Chocolate Oatmeal Drop Cookies 219
Pumpkin-Chocolate Chip Cookies 219
Quick Chewy Bar Cookies 217
Rienzi's Brownies with Fudge Icing 227
Snowflake Spritz Cookies 224
Texas Brownies 226
Tweety's Famous Cookies 218
White Chocolate-Macadamia Chunk Cookies 222
CORN
Butch's Wild West Tex-Mex Salad 87
Cajun Veggie Chili 74
Corn Salad 99
Corn Walnut Dip 23
Creole Corn Chowder Soup 84
Three Corn Casserole 126
Cornish Hens, Glazed with Curried Rice 181
Cowboy Cheddar Soup 77
CRANBERRIES
Brandied Cranberry Sauce 105
Christmas Salad 90
Cranberry Chutney 107
Dried Cranberry and White Chocolate Biscotti 220
Fresh Cranberry Relish 106
Wild Rice and Cranberry Pilaf 132
Cranberry Glogg 50
Crawfish, Spicy Fettuccine with 122
Creamy Artichoke Soup 75
Creamy Baked Chicken Breasts 170
Creamy Basil Dressing 109
Creamy Chicken 175
Crème De Menthe Brownies 225
Creole Corn Chowder Soup 84
Csirke Paprikas Budapest (Chicken Paprika) 179
CUCUMBERS
Chilled Cucumber Soup 73
Gazpacho with Sour Cream 80
Salmon with Cucumber Sauce 185
Cumin Rice 132
Curried Cheese and Olive Spread 25
Curried Chicken Tea Sandwiches 64
Curried Pumpkin Soup 81
Curried Shrimp Salad 97

D

DATES
Date Balls 217
Rose Bowles' Fabulous Fruitcake 201
David's BBQ Shrimp 188
Debbie's Noodle Kugel 120
Debbye's Chicken Log Appetizer 39
DESSERTS *(also see Cakes, Candy, Cookies & Bars, Chocolate, and Pies)*
Apple Bavarian Torte 216
Apricot Whip 191
Aunt Edith's Chocolate Sauce 233
Boiled Custard 200
Chocolate Meringues 232
Chocolate Mint Mousse 208
Frozen Cherry Cream 236
Frozen Lemon Mousse 228
Fudge Sauce for Ice Cream 236
Grandma's Apple Crisp 215
Lemon Curd 221
Meringue Forgetums 234
Mousse au Chocolat 204
Orange Soufflé 237
Oregon Blackberry Meringue Cups 233
Peach Marlow 229
Pears in Red Wine 230
"Ravo" 237
Saratoga Torte 215
Sherried Fruit Compote 231
Sweet Wonton "Napoleon" 235
Tony's Delicious Cheesecake 205
White Wine Granita with Blackberries 231
Diego Rivera Salad 89
Dilled Potato Salad 102
DIPS AND SPREADS *(also see Appetizers)*
Aimee's Artichoke and Sun-Dried Tomato Dip 21
Almond Swiss Cheese Ball 26
Artichoke Dip 21
Baked Brie with Crudités 29

Capanada 36
Chutney Cheese Pâté 33
Corn Walnut Dip 23
Curried Cheese and Olive Spread 25
Debbye's Chicken Log Appetizer 39
Goat Cheese with Sun-Dried Tomatoes and Rosemary 27
Karen's Shrimp Dip 34
My Great Aunt Willimae's King Salmon Mold 37
Olive Nut Spread 24
Pinecone Cheese Ball 26
Shrimp Spread 35
Smoked Oyster Spread 37
"Smoked" Salmon Spread 38
Tapenade Dip 33
Dream Pie 211
Dried Cranberry and White Chocolate Biscotti 220
Dump Coffee Cake 193

E

Easy Chateau Stroganoff 142
Eggnog No. 302 47

EGGPLANT
Capanada 36
Eggplant Moussaka 150
Eggplant, Red Pepper and Feta Gratin 127
Spaghetti with Roasted Eggplant and Tomatoes 117

EGGS
Akuri Spiced Scrambled Eggs 65
Baked Apple French Toast 65
Baked Cushaw 135
Caviar Pie 19
Company's Coming Strata 67
Huevos Rancheros al Pavo 66
Jalapeño Squares 31
Potato Salad Diane 101
Prysnac 66
Quiche without Crust 68
Salmon Soufflé 184

F

Fancy Mustard 104
Festive Party Punch 46
Fettuccine Primavera 115
Filet Mignon 143

FISH
Alexander's Smoked Salmon or Ham Roll-Ups 38
Alison's Salmon 183
Caviar Pie 19
Moules Mariniere (Mussels in White Wine) 182
My Great Aunt Willimae's King Salmon Mold 37
Pirkko's Caviar 19
Salmon Soufflé 184
Salmon with Cucumber Sauce 185
"Smoked" Salmon Spread 38
Southwestern Salmon Spirals 35
Spicy Fettuccine with Crawfish 122
Truites a' l'Ardennaise 184
White Bean Tuna Salad 96
Fix Ahead Mashed Potatoes 131
Flambéed Pepper Steak 145
Four Star Pasta 119
Fran's Coffee Cake 54
French Coffee Cake 57
French Dressing 108
Fresh Cranberry Relish 106
Frosted Beet Soup 79
Frosted Raspberry Salad 105
Frozen Cherry Cream 236
Frozen Lemon Mousse 228
Fudge Pie 209
Fudge Sauce for Ice Cream 236
Fumi Salad 99

G

Gambas al Ajillo 187

GAME
Canard L'Orange (Roast Duck with Oranges) 180
Venison Tenderloin Appetizers 42
Gazpacho 79
Gazpacho with Sour Cream 80
German Chocolate Angel Pie 212
Ginger Almond Tea 46
Glazed Cornish Hens with Curried Rice 181
Goat Cheese with Sun-Dried Tomatoes and Rosemary 27
Gougère with Gruyère Salad 89
Gourmet Pork Filet 162

GRAINS AND CEREALS
No Bake Chocolate Oatmeal Drop Cookies 219
Rich Kentucky Oatmeal Pie 213
Tweety's Famous Cookies 218
Grandma Moses' Gingerbread 196
Grandma's Apple Crisp 215
Grapefruit, Diego Rivera Salad 89
Grapes, Chicken Salad 93
Great Brisket 143
Greek Salad 91
Greek-Style Chicken and Penne Salad 121
Grillades 156
Grilled Asparagus 125

H

Ham-Asparagus Roll-Ups 22
Hash Brown Potato Casserole 129
Hawaiian Chicken Curry 173
Helen Corbitt's Grasshopper Pie 213
Holiday Champagne Punch 44
Honey Puff 70
Hot Chicken Salad 95
Hot Gingered Lemonade 43
Huevos Rancheros al Pavo 66

I

Iced Chocolate and Brandy Creams 206
Italian Zucchini and Tomatoes with Garlic 137

J

Jalapeño Cheese Bites . . . 31
Jalapeño Margaritas . . . 49
Jalapeño Squares . . . 31
Jezebel Sauce . . . 110

K

Kale, Portuguese Kale Soup . . . 76
Karen's Raspberry Cheese Spread . . . 20
Karen's Shrimp Dip . . . 34
Kathryn's Stew . . . 145
Kentucky Christmas Cider . . . 47

L

Lady Finger Mousse Cake . . . 199
LAMB
Lamb and White Bean Ragoût . . . 164
Lamb Shanks à la Merrily . . . 163
Leeks, Mardi Gras Soup . . . 78
Lemon Chess Pie . . . 204
Lemon Curd . . . 221
Lemon Squares . . . 221
Lemony-Light Cooler . . . 48
Leona's Potato Pancakes . . . 130
Lime Pie . . . 210

M

Macaroni and Cheese . . . 118
Macaroni Pastitsio with Phyllo Pastry (Pastilla) . . . 152
Mango Chutney . . . 110
Mardi Gras Soup . . . 78
Margarita Pie . . . 214
Marianna's Mustard Sauce . . . 112
Marian's Luncheon Salad . . . 97
MARINADES
Meat Marinade I . . . 111
Meat Marinade II . . . 111
Pork Marinade . . . 161
Marinated Pork Tenderloin . . . 159
Mary Anne Varner's Little Lizzies . . . 202
Mary Anne Varner's Rococo Chicken . . . 167
Masterson Family Frozen Fruitcake . . . 200
Mayonnaise from Rienzi . . . 112
Meringue Forgetums . . . 234
Microwave Chocolate Peanut Clusters . . . 207
Microwave Pecan Brittle . . . 206
Mint Syrup Concentrate . . . 48
Mocha Pie . . . 209
Moist Meat Loaf . . . 149
Mole de Pollo—Chicken with Peanut Butter Sauce . . . 178
Moules Mariniere (Mussels in White Wine) . . . 182
Mousse au Chocolat . . . 204
Muenster Chicken . . . 169
MUSHROOMS
Chicken Breast in Rum Sauce . . . 168
Chicken with Artichokes . . . 168
Curried Pumpkin Soup . . . 81
Easy Chateau Stroganoff . . . 142
Fettuccine Primavera . . . 115
Gourmet Pork Filet . . . 162
Kathryn's Stew . . . 145
Muenster Chicken . . . 169
Mushroom Stuffing . . . 137
Pickle Mushrooms à la Grecque . . . 24
Spinach and Mushroom Quiche . . . 69
Summer Squash Sauté . . . 134
My Great Aunt Willimae's King Salmon Mold . . . 37

N

No Bake Chocolate Oatmeal Drop Cookies . . . 219
NUTS
Brittle Cracker Cookies . . . 222
Caramel Chocolate Squares . . . 228
Meringue Forgetums . . . 234
Quick Chewy Bar Cookies . . . 217
Rienzi's Brownies with Fudge Icing . . . 227
ALMONDS
Almond Poppy Chicken . . . 171
Almond Swiss Cheese Ball . . . 26
Almond-Lime Loaf . . . 55
Broccoli Cole Slaw . . . 100
Chocolate Meringues . . . 232
Christmas Salad . . . 90
Debbye's Chicken Log Appetizer . . . 39
Fumi Salad . . . 99
Hot Chicken Salad . . . 95
Nutty Wild Rice Salad . . . 92
Oriental Salad . . . 88
"Ravo" . . . 237
Stuffing for Cornish Hens . . . 181
Sybil's Chicken Salad . . . 94
MACADAMIA
White Chocolate-Macadamia Chunk Cookies . . . 222
PEANUTS
Microwave Chocolate Peanut Clusters . . . 207
PECANS
Absolutely Wonderful Sand Tarts . . . 223
Chewy Pecan Pie Squares . . . 234
Chicken and Pecan Rice Salad . . . 98
Chocolate Chip Cake . . . 198
Cinnamon Pecans . . . 205
Dream Pie . . . 211
Dump Coffee Cake . . . 193
Fresh Cranberry Relish . . . 106
Frosted Raspberry Salad . . . 105
Fudge Pie . . . 209
German Chocolate Angel Pie . . . 212
Masterson Family Frozen Fruitcake . . . 200
Microwave Pecan Brittle . . . 206
No Bake Chocolate Oatmeal Drop Cookies . . . 219
Pecan Pie . . . 214
Pinecone Cheese Ball . . . 26
Pralines (from Brennan's) . . . 207
Rose Bowles' Fabulous Fruitcake . . . 201
Swedish Nut Balls . . . 235
The Best Cake (Really) . . . 195
Vanilla Wafer Cake . . . 198
Zack's Cream Cheese Torte . . . 20

Zucchini Bread 62

WALNUTS

Apricot Whip 191
Barbara Lea's Chicken Salad 96
Basil Pesto 108
Brownies 224
Corn Walnut Dip 23
Cranberry Chutney 107
Cranberry Salad 106
Fran's Coffee Cake 54
Saratoga Torte 215

O

OLIVES

Olive Cheese Nuggets 25
Olive Fettuccine 119
Olive Nut Spread 24

ONIONS

Pastelitos 40
Vidalia Onion Pie 126

ORANGES

Canard L'Orange (Roast Duck with Oranges) 180
Christmas Salad 90
Orange Soufflé 237
Oriental Salad 88

Oregon Blackberry Meringue Cups 233
Oriental Salad 88
Orzo Salad 92
Oven Beef Stew 146

OYSTERS, *see Seafood*

P

Passover Sponge Cake 196

PASTA

4 Star Pasta 119
Armenian Pilaf 131
Black Bean, Orzo and Tomato Salad . . . 93
Debbie's Noodle Kugel 120
Easy Chateau Stroganoff 142
Fettuccine Primavera 115
Greek-Style Chicken and Penne Salad 121
Macaroni and Cheese 118
Macaroni Pastitsio with Phyllo Pastry (Pastilla) 152
Olive Fettuccine 119
Orzo Salad 92
Pasta with Sun-Dried Tomatoe 116
Peter Marzio's Famous Lasagna 148
Portofino Primavera 115
Sausage and Mostaccioli Bake 118
Spaghetti with Roasted Eggplant and Tomatoes 117
Spicy Fettuccine with Crawfish 122
Spinach Pasta Shells 116
Stuffed Ziti 117
Texas Stew 146

Pastelitos 40
Patio Potatoes 130
Patrician Peach Pie 212
Peach Marlow 229

PEACHES

Patrician Peach Pie 212
Peach Marlow 229
Sherried Fruit Compote 231

PEARS

Pears in Red Wine 230
Sherried Fruit Compote 231

PEAS, *see Beans and Peas*

PECANS, *see Nuts*

Pepper Jelly 104
Peppery Garlic Shrimp with Sherry Sauce 186
Peter Marzio's Famous Lasagna 148
Pickle Mushrooms à la Grecque 24

PIES *(also see Cakes, Candy, Cookies & Bars, Chocolate, and Desserts)*

Brandy Alexander Pie 210
Chewy Pecan Pie Squares 234
Chocolate Delight Pie 211
Crust 229
Dream Pie 211
Fudge Pie 209
German Chocolate Angel Pie 212
Helen Corbitt's Grasshopper Pie 213
Lemon Chess Pie 204
Lime Pie 210
Margarita Pie 214
Mocha Pie 209
Patrician Peach Pie 212
Pecan Pie 214
Pumpkin Ice Cream Pie 229
Rich Kentucky Oatmeal Pie 213

PINEAPPLE

Barbara Lea's Chicken Salad 96
Dream Pie 211
Frosted Raspberry Salad 105
Frozen Cherry Cream 236
Marian's Luncheon Salad 97
Mary Anne Varner's Little Lizzies 202
Rose Bowles' Fabulous Fruitcake 201
Sherried Fruit Compote 231
Zack's Cream Cheese Torte 20

Pinecone Cheese Ball 26
Pirkko's Caviar 19
Pizza Rustica 32
Poached Chicken with Black Beans and Salsa 174

PORK

BACON

Creole Corn Chowder Soup 84
Oriental Salad 88
Roasted Potato Salad 103
Stuffed Acorn Squash 135
Swiss Tarts 69

HAM

Chicken Pillows for Two 169
Ham-Asparagus Roll-Ups 22
Truites a' l'Ardennaise 184

PORK CHOPS

Ron's Pork Chops 160

ROAST

Spicy Braised Pork 157

Twice-Cooked Pork with Cabbage and Sai Fun 158
SAUSAGE
Cheese Puffs 62
Company's Coming Strata 67
Portuguese Kale Soup 76
Portuguese Soup 77
Sausage and Mostaccioli Bake 118
TENDERLOIN
Gourmet Pork Filet 162
Marinated Pork Tenderloin 159
Pork Tenderloin Medallions 160
Pork Tenderloin with Apple and Red Chile Chutney . . . 161
Pork Marinade 161
Portofino Primavera 115
Portuguese Kale Soup 76
Portuguese Soup 77

POTATOES
Chicken Fricassee 176
Dilled Potato Salad 102
Fix Ahead Mashed Potatoes 131
Hash Brown Potato Casserole 129
Leona's Potato Pancakes 130
Mardi Gras Soup 78
Oven Beef Stew 146
Patio Potatoes 130
Portuguese Kale Soup 76
Portuguese Soup 77
Potato Rolls 60
Potato Salad Diane 101
Potatoes Baked with Tomatoes 128
Roasted Potato Salad 103
Potatoes Baked with Tomatoes 128

POULTRY
CHICKEN
Almond Poppy Chicken 171
Barbara Lea's Chicken Salad 96
Chicken and Pecan Rice Salad 98
Chicken Breast in Rum Sauce 168
Chicken Curry 172
Chicken Enchilada Soup 82
Chicken Enchiladas 170
Chicken Fricassee 176
Chicken Pillows for Two 169
Chicken Salad 93
Chicken Sauté with Fresh Ginger . . . 177
Chicken with Artichokes 168
Creamy Baked Chicken Breasts 170
Creamy Chicken 175
Csirke Paprikas Budapest (Chicken Paprika) 179
Curried Chicken Tea Sandwiches 64
Debbye's Chicken Log Appetizer 39
Greek-Style Chicken and Penne Salad 121
Hawaiian Chicken Curry 173
Hot Chicken Salad 95
Marian's Luncheon Salad 97
Mary Anne Varner's Rococo Chicken . . . 167
Mole de Pollo—Chicken with Peanut Butter Sauce 178
Muenster Chicken 169
Poached Chicken with Black Beans and Salsa 174
Savory Chicken and Asparagus 175
Soft Chicken Tacos 178
Sybil's Chicken Salad 94
Valerie's Tortilla Soup 85
CORNISH HENS
Glazed Cornish Hens with Curried Rice 181
TURKEY
Huevos Rancheros al Pavo 66
Pralines (from Brennan's) 207
Prysnac 66

PUMPKIN
Curried Pumpkin Soup 81
Pumpkin Bread 60
Pumpkin Cake 193
Pumpkin Ice Cream Pie 229
Pumpkin-Chocolate Chip Cookies . . . 219

Q

Quiche without Crust 68
Quick Chewy Bar Cookies 217

R

RAISINS
Cranberry Chutney 107
Fresh Cranberry Relish 106
Mango Chutney 110
Mary Anne Varner's Little Lizzies 202
Masterson Family Frozen Fruitcake . . . 200
RASPBERRIES
Champagne with Raspberries 44
"Ravo" 237
Rhoda's Pound Cake 192
RICE
Armenian Pilaf 131
Chicken and Pecan Rice Salad 98
Chicken Sauté with Fresh Ginger 177
Cumin Rice 132
Glazed Cornish Hens with Curried Rice 181
Jalapeño Cheese Bites 31
Marian's Luncheon Salad 97
Mary Anne Varner's Rococo Chicken . . . 167
Nutty Wild Rice Salad 92
Shrimp Annie 187
Spinach and Rice Casserole 133
Wild Rice and Cranberry Pilaf 132
Rich Kentucky Oatmeal Pie 213
Rick's Waffles 56
Rienzi's Brownies with Fudge Icing 227
Roasted Potato Salad 103
Ron's Pork Chops 160
Rose Bowles' Fabulous Fruitcake 201
Rosemary Damper 61

S

SALAD DRESSINGS
Balsamic Dressing 109
Creamy Basil Dressing 109
Dressing 87, 88, 89, 90, 91, 92, 97, 99, 100

French Dressing . . . 108
Vinaigrette . . . 98

SALADS

Barbara Lea's Chicken Salad . . . 96
Black Bean, Orzo and Tomato Salad . . . 93
Black-Eyed Pea Salad . . . 95
Broccoli Cole Slaw . . . 100
Butch's Wild West Tex-Mex Salad . . . 87
Chicken and Pecan Rice Salad . . . 98
Chicken Salad . . . 93
Christmas Salad . . . 90
Confetti Cole Slaw . . . 100
Corn Salad . . . 99
Curried Shrimp Salad . . . 97
Diego Rivera Salad . . . 89
Dilled Potato Salad . . . 102
Frosted Raspberry Salad . . . 105
Fumi Salad . . . 99
Gougère with Gruyère Salad . . . 89
Greek Salad . . . 91
Greek-Style Chicken and Penne Salad . . . 121
Hot Chicken Salad . . . 95
Marian's Luncheon Salad . . . 97
Nutty Wild Rice Salad . . . 92
Oriental Salad . . . 88
Orzo Salad . . . 92
Potato Salad Diane . . . 101
Roasted Potato Salad . . . 103
Shrimp Salad . . . 86
Spinach Salad . . . 90
Sybil's Chicken Salad . . . 94
Tabbouleh . . . 91
Tex-Mex Marinated Salad . . . 86
Virginia's Tomato Aspic . . . 103
White Bean Tuna Salad . . . 96

SALMON

Alexander's Smoked Salmon or Ham Roll-Ups . . . 38
Alison's Salmon . . . 183
My Great Aunt Willimae's King Salmon Mold . . . 37
Salmon Soufflé . . . 184
Salmon with Cucumber Sauce . . . 185
"Smoked" Salmon Spread . . . 38
Southwestern Salmon Spirals . . . 35

Salsa . . . 174
Sandwiches, Curried Chicken Tea . . . 64
Sangría . . . 49
Saratoga Torte . . . 215

SAUCES AND SEASONINGS

Basil Pesto . . . 108
Béchamel Sauce . . . 151
Marianna's Mustard Sauce . . . 112
Meat Marinade I . . . 111
Meat Marinade II . . . 111
Sauce for Salmon . . . 183, 185
White Sauce . . . 171

Sausage and Mostaccioli Bake . . . 118
Savory Chicken and Asparagus . . . 175

SEAFOOD

OYSTERS

Smoked Oyster Spread . . . 37

SHRIMP

Curried Shrimp Salad . . . 97
David's BBQ Shrimp . . . 188
Gambas al Ajillo . . . 187
Karen's Shrimp Dip . . . 34
Peppery Garlic Shrimp with Sherry Sauce . . . 186
Shrimp Annie . . . 187
Shrimp de Jonghe . . . 34
Shrimp Salad . . . 86
Shrimp Spread . . . 35

Seven-Up Cake . . . 201
Sherried Fruit Compote . . . 231
"Smoked" Salmon Spread . . . 38
Snowflake Spritz Cookies . . . 224
Soft Chicken Tacos . . . 178

SOUPS AND STEWS

Aimee's Bombay Chiller . . . 73
Amy's Brie Soup . . . 78
Cajun Veggie Chili . . . 74
Calabacitas (Cream of Squash Soup) . . . 80
Chicken Enchilada Soup . . . 82
Chilled Cucumber Soup . . . 73
Cowboy Cheddar Soup . . . 77
Creamy Artichoke Soup . . . 75
Creole Corn Chowder Soup . . . 84
Curried Pumpkin Soup . . . 81
Frosted Beet Soup . . . 79
Gazpacho . . . 79
Gazpacho with Sour Cream . . . 80
Kathryn's Stew . . . 145
Mardi Gras Soup . . . 78
Oven Beef Stew . . . 146
Portuguese Kale Soup . . . 76
Portuguese Soup . . . 77
Spiced Broth . . . 76
Taos Society Soup (Roasted Red Pepper Soup) . . . 83
Texas Stew . . . 146
Valerie's Tortilla Soup . . . 85

Southwestern Dressing . . . 138
Southwestern Salmon Spirals . . . 35
Spaghetti with Roasted Eggplant and Tomatoes . . . 117
Sparkling Strawberry Punch . . . 50
Spiced Broth . . . 76
Spicy Braised Pork . . . 157
Spicy Fettuccine with Crawfish . . . 122

SPINACH

Baked Spinach Square . . . 28
Cajun Veggie Chili . . . 74
Pastelitos . . . 40
Spinach and Mushroom Quiche . . . 69
Spinach and Rice Casserole . . . 133
Spinach Casserole . . . 133
Spinach Pasta Shells . . . 116
Spinach Roll . . . 63
Spinach Salad . . . 90

SQUASH

Baked Cushaw . . . 135
Calabacitas . . . 134
Calabacitas (Cream of Squash Soup) . . . 80
Stuffed Acorn Squash . . . 135

Summer Squash Sauté 134
Yellow Squash and Cornbread Casserole 136
Yellow Squash Patties 136

STRAWBERRIES
Cake Roll 203
Sparkling Strawberry Punch 50
Strawberry Bread 61
Sweet Wonton "Napoleon" 235

Stuffed Acorn Squash 135
Stuffed Ziti 117
Stuffing 181
Summer Squash Sauté 134
Swedish Nut Balls 235
Sweet and Sour Cabbage Rolls 153
Sweet 'n' Sour Asparagus 125

SWEET POTATOES
Sweet Potato Biscuits 59
Sweet Potato Soufflé 129

Sweet Wonton "Napoleon" 235
Swiss Tarts 69
Sybil's Chicken Salad 94

T

Tabbouleh 91
Taos Society Soup (Roasted Red Pepper Soup) 83
Tapenade Dip 33
Teriyaki 144
Tex-Mex Marinated Salad 86
Texas Brownies 226
Texas Caviar 30
Texas Stew 146
The Best Chocolate Cake 197
Three Corn Casserole 126

TOMATOES
4 Star Pasta 119
Black Bean, Orzo and Tomato Salad 93
Butch's Wild West Tex-Mex Salad 87
Cajun Veggie Chili 74
Creole Corn Chowder Soup 84
Csirke Paprikas Budapest (Chicken Paprika) 179
Eggplant Moussaka 150
Gazpacho with Sour Cream 80
Goat Cheese with Sun-Dried Tomatoes and Rosemary 27
Greek Salad 91
Italian Zucchini and Tomatoes with Garlic 137
Lamb and White Bean Ragoût 164
Macaroni Pastitsio with Phyllo Pastry (Pastilla) 152
Pasta with Sun-Dried Tomatoes 116
Peter Marzio's Famous Lasagna 148
Portofino Primavera 115
Portuguese Kale Soup 76
Portuguese Soup 77
Potatoes Baked with Tomatoes 128
Salsa 174
Soft Chicken Tacos 178
Spaghetti with Roasted Eggplant and Tomatoes 117
Tabbouleh 91
Texas Caviar 30
Texas Stew 146
Valerie's Tortilla Soup 85
Virginia's Tomato Aspic 103

Tony's Delicious Cheesecake 205
Tortilla Roll-Ups 30
Truites a' l'Ardennaise 184

TURKEY, *see Poultry*

Turnip Soufflé 138
Tweety's Famous Cookies 218
Twice-Cooked Pork with Cabbage and Sai Fun 158

V

Valerie's Tortilla Soup 85
Vanilla Wafer Cake 198

VEAL
Grillades 156
Veal Cutlets Parmesan 154
Zurich Geschnetzeltes (Veal) 155

Venison Tenderloin Appetizers 42
Vidalia Onion Pie 126
Virginia's Tomato Aspic 103

W

WALNUTS, *see Nuts*

WATERFOWL
Canard L'Orange (Roast Duck with Oranges) 180

White Bean Tuna Salad 96
White Chocolate-Macadamia Chunk Cookies 222
White Sauce 171
White Wine Granita with Blackberries . . 231
Wild Rice and Cranberry Pilaf 132

Y

Yellow Squash and Cornbread Casserole 136
Yellow Squash Patties 136

Z

Zack's Cream Cheese Torte 20

ZUCCHINI
Calabacitas 134
Italian Zucchini and Tomatoes with Garlic 137
Marinated Pork Tenderloin 159
Portofino Primavera 115
Summer Squash Sauté 134
Zucchini Bread 62
Zucchini Nibbles 23

Zurich Geschnetzeltes (Veal) 155

The Guild Collection:
Recipes from Art Lovers

Please send ______ copies of *THE GUILD COLLECTION* @ $19.95 each $________

Texas residents add 8 1/4% sales tax (or current tax rate) $________

Shipping and Handling @ $6.95 $________

Total $________

Ship To:

Name ________________________ Phone ______________

Address ______________________________________

City ____________________ State ______ Zip Code ____________

Method of Payment: ☐ Check ☐ Credit Card

Please make checks payable to The MFAH

The MFAH • Attention: Bookstore
P.O. Box 6826 • Houston, Texas 77265 • 713-639-7360

Visa/MasterCard/American Express Card Number ______________________

Signature ________________________ Expiration Date ____________

Credit card orders may be placed by calling 713-639-7365 or fax 713-639-7710

Proceeds from the sale of this book will go to the Guild's continuing support of programs at The Museum of Fine Arts, Houston

The Guild Collection:
Recipes from Art Lovers

Please send ______ copies of *THE GUILD COLLECTION* @ $19.95 each $________

Texas residents add 8 1/4% sales tax (or current tax rate) $________

Shipping and Handling @ $6.95 $________

Total $________

Ship To:

Name ________________________ Phone ______________

Address ______________________________________

City ____________________ State ______ Zip Code ____________

Method of Payment: ☐ Check ☐ Credit Card

Please make checks payable to The MFAH

The MFAH • Attention: Bookstore
P.O. Box 6826 • Houston, Texas 77265 • 713-639-7360

Visa/MasterCard/American Express Card Number ______________________

Signature ________________________ Expiration Date ____________

Credit card orders may be placed by calling 713-639-7365 or fax 713-639-7710

Proceeds from the sale of this book will go to the Guild's continuing support of programs at The Museum of Fine Arts, Houston